UNBURDENED

A Message to the Pulpits of America

Caleb J. Breedlove

TBG Studio Press
Tulsa, OK

Published by
TBG Studio Press, a subsidiary of TBG Holding Co.

For permission requests, write to the publisher, addressed "Attention: Permissions Coordinator," at the address below.

Unburdened: A Message to the Pulpits of America/Caleb J. Breedlove. – 2nd ed.
ISBN: 979-8-9944345-2-9

Contents

I dedicate this book to God, The Holy Spirit. May your voice be heard in the heart of every reader.

The Power of The Gospel and The Holy Spirit to Overcome

Beloved fellow servants in Christ's vineyard,

I write these words with a heart overflowing with gratitude for the boundless grace, patience, and kindness of our God. The content that follows was penned over ten years ago, birthed from a season of intense spiritual burden and prophetic urgency. Yet as I prepare to share these messages with you, I feel compelled by the Holy Spirit to first open my heart about the journey that has brought me to this moment.

When I first wrote these chapters, I carried within my soul a burning conviction about the state of American pulpits. The words flowed with prophetic fire, yet I confess to you now that in the midst of delivering with this prophetic burden, I wrestled with my own spiritual poverty. Pride, that ancient enemy of every preacher, had entangled my heart more deeply than I dared to admit. Even as I penned warnings about lukewarmness and prayerlessness, I found myself trapped in cycles of spiritual defeat that left me questioning whether I was qualified to speak such things.

The years that followed were marked by seasons of profound depression, overwhelming life challenges, and the kind of soul-searching that strips away every pretense. There were moments when the weight of these prophetic words felt crushing—not because they were untrue, but because I knew how desperately I needed their message in my own life. How could I call others to holiness when I struggled to maintain it? How could I speak of the power of prayer when my own prayer life felt mechanical and distant?

It was in this valley of spiritual poverty that I discovered the profound truth Dallas Willard expressed so beautifully: "Jesus does not call us to do what he did, but to be as he was, permeated with love. Then the doing of what he did and said becomes the natural expression of who we are in him."[1] For years, I had approached the call to "be perfect" as Christ commanded as another mountainous task I must accomplish through sheer spiritual effort. I had missed the glorious reality that perfection, holiness, and the abundant life are not achievements but surrenders—not my striving toward Christlikeness, but Christ's life flowing through me.

In His mercy, the Lord led me into a season of deep spiritual formation that encompassed not only classical spiritual disciplines but also the healing ministries of professional therapy, emotional health counseling, and spiritual direction. I learned that the God who commands us to "work out your salvation with fear and trembling" is the same God who promises that "it is God who works in you both to will and to do for His good pleasure." The fear and trembling is not about our ability to perform righteousness, but about our willingness to yield completely to His transforming work within us.

Through this season of breaking and rebuilding, I experienced what Willard called the true aim of spiritual formation: "not behavior modification but the transformation of all those aspects of you and me where behavior comes from—circumcision of the heart."[2] I discovered that surrender is not defeat but victory—not the end of my efforts but the beginning of His supernatural work through me. The life I now live, I live by faith in the Son of God who loved me and gave Himself for me. Every day I am learning anew that Christ in me is not merely a theological concept but a living, breathing reality that transforms every aspect of existence.

This revelation has revolutionized my understanding of ministry and calling. No longer do I strive to be a perfect vessel; instead, I yield to become an available vessel. The Holy Spirit does not need my perfection—He needs my surrender. He does not require my strength—He desires my weakness so that His power may be made perfect. As Willard wisely observed, "When we receive God's gift of life by relying on Christ, we find that God comes to act with us as we rely on him in our actions."[3]

Fellow servants, as you read these chapters, I want you to remember the tender words of Christ to the church in Ephesus: "I know your works, your labor, your patience, and that you cannot bear those who are evil... Nevertheless I have this against you, that you have left your first love."[4] Oh, how these words pierce the heart! Here was a church commended for their doctrinal purity, their hard work, and their unwillingness to tolerate falsehood. Yet they had drifted from what mattered most—their passionate love for Jesus Himself.

Christ's counsel to them is His counsel to us: "Remember therefore from where you have fallen; repent and do the first works."[5] This is not a call to try harder or do more, but to return to the simplicity and purity of devotion to Christ. It is an invitation to rediscover that place where ministry flows not from duty but from delight, not from obligation but from overwhelming love.

I have learned that the greatest enemy of authentic ministry is not opposition from without but the slow drift of the heart within—when our zeal for success eclipses our zeal for the Savior, when our passion for leadership overshadows our passion for the Lord, when our desire for influence becomes greater than our desire for intimacy with the Infinite. These are subtle seductions that can capture even the most sincere servants.

But here is the glorious news—the same Christ who exposes our poverty is the Christ who fills our emptiness. The same Spirit who convicts us of our desperate need is the Spirit who empowers us for supernatural living. The gospel is not merely the good news of our forgiveness; it is the good news of our transformation. We are not just forgiven sinners hoping to muddle through until heaven; we are being transformed into the very image of Christ by the Spirit of the living God.

As you engage with these prophetic words in the coming chapters, I encourage you to receive them not as condemnation but as an invitation—an invitation to return to your first love, to rediscover the joy of your salvation, to experience afresh the wonder of walking with Jesus. These messages are not meant to crush your spirit but to awaken it, not to discourage your heart but to set it ablaze with holy passion.

The Church in America stands at a crossroads. We can continue down the path of religious activity without spiritual vitality, or we can humble ourselves before the throne of grace and cry out for a fresh visitation of the Holy Spirit. We can persist in our own strength and wisdom, or we can surrender to the transforming power of the gospel that makes all things new.

My prayer is that these words will find fertile soil in hearts hungry for more of God. May they serve not as a weapon of judgment but as a tool of grace, not as a source of guilt but as a catalyst for glory. And may we all discover together what it means to be so captured by Christ that our lives become walking demonstrations of His beauty, power, and love.

The same Jesus who walked on water still walks among His churches today. He still speaks to those who have ears to hear. He still transforms those who have hearts to yield. May we be found among the faithful when He appears, not because we have achieved perfection, but because we have surrendered to the Perfect One who delights to live His life through surrendered vessels.

Come, let us return to our first love. Come, let us rediscover the wonder of walking with God. Come, let us be vessels through whom the life of Jesus flows into a world desperate for His touch. The hour is late, but His mercies are new every morning. There is yet time for revival, yet hope for restoration, yet opportunity for the Church to arise and shine with the glory of her Lord.

With deep affection and holy expectation in Christ,
Caleb

Endnotes

1. Dallas Willard, quoted in "Dallas Willard Quotes," Goodreads. Willard's insight captures the essence of authentic Christian living—not mere imitation of Jesus's actions but participation in His very nature and being.

2. Dallas Willard, Renovation of the Heart: Putting On the Character of Christ (Colorado Springs: NavPress, 2002). Willard consistently emphasized that true spiritual formation targets the heart—the source from which all behavior flows.

3. Dallas Willard, The Divine Conspiracy: Rediscovering Our Hidden Life in God (San Francisco: Harper Collins, 1998). This quote captures the mystery of cooperation with divine grace—God acting with us as we rely upon Him.

4. Revelation 2:2-4 (NKJV). Christ's commendation and rebuke to the church at Ephesus reveals how it's possible to maintain doctrinal orthodoxy and ministerial activity while losing the essential element—passionate love for Jesus Himself.

5. Revelation 2:5 (NKJV). Christ's call to remember, repent, and return to the "first works" emphasizes that restoration begins with recalling our former devotion and taking concrete steps to rekindle our love relationship with Him.

Prologue

The consuming passion of my life is given to the gospel of the kingdom and its advancement throughout the nations. I find myself in the secret place, deeply moved, *"labor[ing] in birth...until Christ is formed in you"* (Gal. 4:19). As I sow myself deeper into prayer for the body of Christ—its maturity and function in the world—I become ever so grieved at her condition. I am saddened with my brothers and sisters who have forsaken the true gospel of Christ, forfeiting it for the so-called great news of unbiblical grace. With *"itching ears, [we have] heap[ed] up for [our]selves teachers;...[we have] turn[ed our] ears away from the truth,...to fables"* (2 Tim. 4:3–4).[1]

As we approach the appearance of Christ, His question rings in my spirit:

"Nevertheless, when the Son of Man comes, will He really find faith on the earth?" (Luke 18:8)

Will He find a people that know Him? Will He find a people that have heard His gospel? I am not sure of it.[2] The gospel today preaches grace unto happiness, without the cross unto holiness.[3] Today's gospel preaches affectionate love and comfort without preaching repentance unto transformation. Many are dying without hearing the true gospel of Christ's cross and coming kingdom. They hear the message of *"say a prayer and try to do better,"* but the gospel that saves souls is about Christ's death, burial, and resurrection—and thus the death and burial of our old life and our resurrection to come. The gospel that saves souls is complete trust in the name of Jesus and the power and ministry of His Holy Spirit.

Many are calling on the name of the preachers but not on the name of the Lord. As Romans 10 professes, *"How then shall they call on Him in whom they have not believed? And how shall they believe in Him of whom they have not heard? And how shall they hear without a preacher?"* (Rom. 10:14). Not just any *preacher*—but preachers of the true gospel of Christ.[4] Preachers that pray and proclaim messages that rest not on the arm of the flesh but on *"the demonstration of the Spirit and of power, that your faith should not be in the wisdom of men but in the power of God"* (1 Cor. 2:4–5). I believe God is calling, redeeming, and preparing such preachers again.[5]

Endnotes

1. The reference here is to 2 Timothy 4:3–4 (NKJV): *"For the time will come when they will not endure sound doctrine, but according to their own desires, because they have itching ears, they will heap up for themselves teachers; and they will turn their ears away from the truth, and be turned aside to fables."* Paul's warning to Timothy about the church's condition in the last days remains urgently relevant.

2. Leonard Ravenhill observed, *"The Church right now has more fashion than passion, is more pathetic than prophetic, is more superficial than supernatural."* Leonard Ravenhill, *Revival God's Way* (Minneapolis: Bethany House, 1983), 57.

3. Dietrich Bonhoeffer's warning against this very danger remains prophetic: *"Cheap grace is the preaching of forgiveness without requiring repentance, baptism without church discipline, Communion without confession.... Cheap grace is grace without discipleship, grace without the cross, grace without Jesus Christ, living and incarnate."* Dietrich Bonhoeffer, *The Cost of Discipleship* (New York: Macmillan, 1959), 45.

4. Ravenhill's charge to preachers is convicting: *"No man is greater than his prayer life. The pastor who is not praying is playing; the people who are not praying are straying. We have many organizers, but few agonizers; many players and payers, few pray-ers; many singers, few clingers; lots of pastors, few wrestlers; many fears, few tears; much fashion, little passion; many interferers, few intercessors; many writers, but few fighters. Failing here, we fail everywhere."* Leonard Ravenhill, *Why Revival Tarries* (Minneapolis: Bethany House, 2004), 23.

5. A.W. Tozer likewise warned, *"It is my opinion that tens of thousands of people, if not millions, have been brought into some kind of religious experience by accepting Christ, and they have not been saved."* Quoted in Ray Comfort, *God Has a Wonderful Plan for Your Life* (Bellflower, CA: Living Waters Publications, 2010), 14. Ravenhill adds, *"I believe God is calling and preparing such preachers again. Without question, the greatest need of this hour is that the church shall meet her ascended Lord again, and get an enduement that would usher in the revival of revivals just before the night of nights settles over this age of incomparable corruption."* Leonard Ravenhill, *Why Revival Tarries*, 19.

Purging the Pulpit

"Within this coming time, there is a holy confrontation or-dained for the Church. The Lord is visiting our churches, sit-ting in our pews, listening to our messages, for the plumb line has been sent from heaven, and the vinedresser is here to judge our fruit and fruitfulness."

In August 2015, in a prayer meeting, the Lord brought forth that prophetic word. As I spoke it, conviction was heavy, and a great urgency unto repentance began to rise in our hearts and mouths. Our hearts were broken as the Lord began en-lightening us about our condition. And the first thing that came from my spirit in repentance was for our preaching and preachers. Upon my knees, I began to repent before the Lord because we had allowed the enemy in.

Family, we have allowed the serpent to sit with us in our pews and preach from our pulpits. Doctrines of devils are spo-ken forth freely and without correction or analysis, for they come out of the mouths of those who have mastered influ-ence.[1] Doctrines of devils have seeped into the fabric of series-driven pastors that no longer search and study the word of truth, but instead seek the excitement and *"encouragement"* of the crowd. Preachers that no longer persevere with the doc-trines of truth for they are not marketable. We have heaped for ourselves preachers with dim eyes and fat hearts, comfortable in lives of sin and compromise but permitted to continue in their positions because of their charisma and talents—void of heartfelt repentance and righteous living.[2]

These men and women have no fear of the Lord. They have no reverence for the price of salvation, so much so that they have seemingly too easily forgotten to preach His name—even pray in His name. We have so-called ministers of a gospel simply not represented in the word of God. We have ministers that deny the deity of Christ and the present ministry of the Holy Spirit. Preachers not denying Jesus outright, but surely dethroning Him. We have heaped for ourselves anti-Christ preachers. Yes, for they have neglected to proclaim His gospel because it requires too much of the sinner. As Dietrich Bonhoeffer expressed, the preachers of today are proclaimers of cheap grace, cheap salvation, cheap prayers, cheap gifts—and they are cheap because we have deemed them and bestowed them upon ourselves.[3]

Family, we are in crisis. We are lacking preachers that have been blessed by God, and we have gathered ourselves around masters of social media who walk hand in hand with the world. We are deceived, for we have allowed water to be poured on the fires of truth and we have allowed dissension and disunity in our camps as we wrap ourselves in the silks of peace with strangers to God and have forsaken the robe of righteousness.[4]

Family, this crisis is heavily upon their actions and upon us as well, for we have talked about them, we have been vexed by them, yet we are silent—yet we have allowed them to represent us. The guilt is upon our heads as well, for our silence is permission and our passivity is their affirmation to continue against the ways of God. And judgment is promised for this. Yes, the harvest of our wickedness and deeds are the cause of our great turmoil and the lack of fruit. For our representatives have lessened our witness amongst the world and they see us as kindred. Oh sure, there is still persecution—nevertheless, the movement unto peace with strangers to God rises to make the bond of friendship to end the persecution. And in our silence, in our passivity, in our slumber and ungodly forbearance, we have become part of that movement.

There were preachers like this in the chronicles of Kings in which the judgment of God came without mercy. The first pair in 1 Kings were prophets—prophets of the god of this world. They worshiped Baal, the ancient god of the Canaanites. They called Baal the lord of good fortune and the lord of wealth; to them Baal was the giver of welfare to those that were worshippers and the destructor of the opposing. They worshipped him through sacrifices of sexual immorality, religious prostitution, and harm to self in the name of worship to Baal.

Oh, you might say, "Caleb, this sounds nothing like today's preachers." Oh, but it does. The same practices run wild amongst "our" preachers that proclaim the name of the Lord but in dark and hidden places give themselves to scandalous wickedness. We know this because of their lax approach to the topic of sin. We know this because there are those that give themselves to lifestyles dedicated to the practice of sin and still find it easy to preach in the name of Jesus, perverting the word of God to indulge in their compromise. Oh, the preachers of Baal are still around. They worship wealth and they are fat in the gospel of good fortune.[5]

Does Christ want us prosperous? Yes, but not at the cost of righteousness, not at the cost of holiness, not at the cost of His gospel for our comfort and well-being. These preachers, though they proclaim to be followers of Christ, have no cross on their back. They know not the crucifixion of sinfulness within their lives. These preachers wallow in the cesspool of their own iniquity while simultaneously justifying it in the excuses of human imperfection and the hall-pass of grace, preaching the foolishness of permissible wickedness. Oh, they are not preachers of the cross of Christ if they are not wearing one in their lives and modeling a life of holiness and separation unto the Lord.[6]

Judgment came to these preachers of Baal through a revelation of God by demonstration of His power. Elijah, God's preacher, came and proclaimed to God's people that (through their silence) bowed the same knee to Baal:

"How long will you falter between two opinions? If the Lord is God, follow Him; but if Baal, follow him." (1 Kings 18:21)

Family, this is the same question I pose to you: How long will we stay double-minded? How long will we allow the poison of the enemy to infect the DNA of our mission in the earth through those that we have allowed to speak for us? How long will we stand compromised yet seeking the benefits of God? Wanting and walking in the ways of the world while awaiting the salvation of the Lord. It cannot be so. We cannot waver between two masters. We must hate one and love the other. Yet preachers that preach in the name of Christ say we can. It is a lie and it will lead us to hell.[7]

These preachers are path-pavers who are not in favor with the straight and narrow—the path that leads only to Christ. They are paving a wide path. They are paving the highway to hell and eternal separation from the Lord. For the word of God commands and calls for holiness, separation from the ways and pleasures of the world unto God's ways and pleasures, for Scripture declares, *"Pursue peace with all people, and holiness, without which no one will see the Lord"* (Heb. 12:14). We must choose. I must and you must. We must belong to one way. In the early days of Christianity, we were not called Christians or Christ-ones; we were called, *"Those who belong to The Way"* (Acts 9:2).[8] Think about that: the world knew us by our unified decision that whoever we were and wherever they found us, they knew—that is one who belonged to *The Way*. Not two ways, not one of the ways—*The Way*.

Elijah continues by demanding a difference to be made between Baal and the one and only True God. He declares:

"Call on the name of your gods, and I will call on the name of the Lord; and the God who answers by fire, He is God." (1 Kings 18:24)

He says, let us put these two opinions to the test. The Christ of the Bible and the christ of our own compromised interpretations are different. Jesus Christ, the one of the Bible, is fully God in a human body. He was conceived and birthed by a virgin, lived a sinless life, ministered as the Lord and Savior of all humanity present and to come. By the Spirit of God upon Him, He healed the sick and raised the dead. He taught the truth with authority and showed grace unto righteousness and holiness before God. He gave Himself unto death that we might be freed from our penalty of sin, which was death unto hell. He endured a horrific death, went to a horrific hell for us, won the horrific fight over salvation and took the keys of authority of death and hell from the god of this world, and by the power of His Father who sent Him, He was raised from the dead.

He ascended to sit at the right hand of His Father, to earnestly pray that we all would believe in Him unto salvation, for His heart is that we repent from our wickedness and enter into His fellowship and live a right-standing and holy life before God. He now awaits as the worthy Lord, for all things to be submitted to Him and to judge us all—those who belong to The Way and those who have rejected it—according to our words and deeds before Him. He is The Only Way unto salvation, The Only Way unto freedom, The Only Way unto healing, The Only Way unto life after our physical body dies, The Only Way unto eternity in pure unfeigned bliss with the Father. He is the only name that has been given to men, that we might believe and be saved from living an eternity in a burning, punishing, miserable hell. That is the Christ of the Bible. That is the only Christ that men can believe on and call on unto salvation, healing, freedom, grace, mercy, holiness, and righteousness unto eternity with Him in pure unrelenting joy and security. But the christ of this age is not the Christ. The christ we have created is only one opinion unto happiness, he is one way unto heaven, he is only one option unto freedom. He offers grace without requiring righteous living. This christ is not condemning, but he has already saved all persons, so we can do what we want and live however we want because his forbearance with us allows for such. This christ did not do any miracles, he died and was not resurrected. This christ was simply one of the many teachers. He is not fairer than Muhammad, or Buddha, or Confucius. This christ is only an impersonator of the qualities and scriptures that we have twisted and taken out of context that we might find rest in our homosexuality, adultery, idolatry—and do not forget our religious fornication.[9]

This christ allows us to hate, be greedy, gossip, lie, and cheat. This christ tolerates our addictions to pornography and our half-hearted repentance. This christ, the christ we have created for ourselves, demands nothing but *"good"* living void of self-denial and filled with indulgences. This christ only gives but does not take away. This christ tolerates drunkenness, jealousy, self-ambition, anger, revenge, and all other kinds of what we call *"mere human imperfections."* So you can see, the Christ of the Bible is not the christ we have allowed to represent us. Oh no, we think we follow the same christ but we do not. The Jesus that is being preached by many preachers today is not the Jesus of the Bible. He is an impersonator, a mere form empty of the substance of the true resurrected Christ.

The people under Elijah's preaching were torn between two opinions. They could not distinguish who was God. And like them, we today have the same struggle within our ranks. The same poison flowing in the messages of our pulpits in America. Oh yes, the god of this world has played his cards right and captured men and women that probably once belonged to The Way and poisoned them with the pleasures of this world. And because we have allowed them to represent us and preach in the name of our Christ, we now struggle to distinguish the true Christ.

Scripture says that the preachers of Baal began to call on their god crying, "O Baal, hear us!" It says, *"they cried aloud, and cut themselves, as was their custom"* (1 Kings 18:28). But there was no answer. They even continued to preach and prophesy that their god was real, *"but there was no voice; no one answered, no one paid attention"* (1 Kings 18:29). The difference between them and us is that they were further away from eternity than we are.

The preachers of Baal today preach a christ our sin created, and they prophesy in his name, and give big testimonies and offerings in his name—yet when they reach eternity assured to see this christ they are so convinced and so convincing of, they will meet their deceiver. They will stand before God together, and He will accuse them of leaving and rejecting the Way for their own bodily pleasures. They will stand before the real Christ and plead for His mercy and His grace that they neglected to preach. They will plead amongst all of their followers that believed in their *"gospel"* and cry out for the true grace unto salvation, freedom, and eternal prosperity. They will say to Him:

"Lord, Lord, have we not prophesied in Your name, cast out demons in Your name, and done many wonders in Your name?"

And they will hear the thunderous and daunting words of the true Christ:

"I never knew you; depart from Me, you who practice lawlessness!" (Matt. 7:22–23)

They will cry, and plead, and demand another chance to do it again—to go back and preach the true gospel, to be resurrected with the same power they rejected. They will wail and bow low as the sheriff of eternity drags them out of the courtroom of heaven and throws them and their followers into the second death. The death of which there is no return.[10]

Brother, will you be counted amongst these preachers? Sister, will you continue in your own way and not turn to The Way? Family, will you not see that the christ that we have made to cope with our sins has left us empty? Can you not see that you are truly not free? For what kind of life is it to gain the entire world with its pleasures and lose your own soul? Friend, you may be happy in your compromise, and you may enjoy the affections of fleeting pleasures—yet is your soul really secured? Are you serving a christ you made up or the true Christ? Family, we are not set free unless we have been forgiven of our offenses before God, through His Son who is the true Christ. We must believe on and call on the only name, the only way, the only truth, our only redemption—Jesus Christ of the Bible.

Elijah, after the preachers of Baal came up empty within themselves and their beliefs, built an altar to the Lord. When he had prepared it, he called on the name that saves and heals. He called on the only name by which salvation, freedom, and eternal prosperity appears. He called on the name of the one Savior, The Only Way, and there was an answer. The preachers of Baal called on the name of their false god and there was no life, no answer, no voice, nothing. But when Elijah called on the name of the Lord, He answered—and He answered demonstratively. A pillar of fire came from the sky in response to the cry of His servant. He lives unlike the false god of the other preachers. He lives to save and heal. He lives to set free.

Think of the revival of hope and faith as the people were no longer torn between two opinions. Scripture states that now assured, "they fell on their faces; and they said, 'The Lord, He is God! The Lord, He is God!'" (1 Kings 18:39). After Elijah prayed, *"Hear me, O Lord, hear me, that this people may know that You are the Lord God, and that You have turned their hearts back to You again"* (1 Kings 18:37)—fire came and responded before all the preachers of the false god and before all the wavering people and ended the controversy.

The great scandal was answered. The Lord, who is holy and righteous altogether, is God—and He is powerful to save. God did not just end the controversy in the souls of His people, but after three years of drought, this same God responded again to the prayers of His servant and sent heavy rain that healed the land of its reign of decay. He sent fire before the rain. The people repented and turned their hearts to the Lord, and *then* He sent forth rain.[11]

Today, it seems many want the rain before the fire. We want the gifts of refreshing to quench the thirsts of our souls yet without fire, without being purified. But today, as the curtains of eternity are near their unraveling, fire is needed. The fire that proves the genuineness of our faith. The fire that frees us from the chains of worldly pleasure. The fire that burns the veil that keeps us from seeing the real Christ. We need the fire that fills us with zealousness for the King and strips us from our selfish ambition unto a deep-seated conviction and fear of the Lord residing in our very bones. We need the Lord's fire to fall upon our congregation, upon our preachers. Oh, that the Lord may purge our pulpits![12]

The Lord is confronting us, family. He is requiring us to show the fruit of our dealings in His name. He is sitting in your pews, listening to your messages, judging whether or not you are worthy of the last outpouring. He is giving you another chance to turn from the christ that our sin has created and turn to the real Christ of the Bible. There is an opportunity to return to the fellowship of salvation and leave the abuses of grace behind. In His kindness He has sent this message to you that you may turn to Him again and preach His gospel: *"Repent, for the kingdom of heaven is at hand!"* (Matt. 4:17).

Will you leave your ways and become one who belongs to The Way? Will you leave the highway unto hell that you have helped to create and return to the straight and narrow gate where our redemption awaits? Will you pick up your cross, deny yourself, and by the power and guidance of the Holy Spirit follow the true Christ? Will you, preacher? Will you, pastor? Will you, evangelist? Will you, prophet? Will you, teacher? Will you, apostle? Will you return?

For if you do not, mercy will not be able to reach you in eternity. Let not the enemy harden your hearts and deceive you to fight for your christ. Believe in the Gospel of Christ again, repent of your sins, and yield to the grace unto holiness and righteousness before the Lord.

He who has an ear to hear, let him hear what the Spirit says.

Endnotes

1. Paul warned Timothy of this very condition: *"Now the Spirit expressly says that in latter times some will depart from the faith, giving heed to deceiving spirits and doctrines of demons, speaking lies in hypocrisy, having their own conscience seared with a hot iron"* (1 Tim. 4:1–2 NKJV).

2. A.W. Tozer observed, *"The contemporary moral climate does not favor a faith as tough and fibrous as that taught by our Lord and His apostles.... And the fault lies with our leaders. They are too timid to tell the people all the truth. They are now asking men to give to God that which costs them nothing."* A.W. Tozer, *God Tells the Man Who Cares* (Harrisburg, PA: Christian Publications, 1970), 62.

3. See Dietrich Bonhoeffer, *The Cost of Discipleship* (New York: Macmillan, 1959), 45–47. Bonhoeffer writes, *"Cheap grace is the preaching of forgiveness without requiring repentance, baptism without church discipline, Communion without confession.... Cheap grace is grace without discipleship, grace without the cross, grace without Jesus Christ, living and incarnate."*

4. Tozer declared, *"We are not diplomats but prophets, and our message is not a compromise but an ultimatum."* A.W. Tozer, *Of God and Men* (Harrisburg, PA: Christian Publications, 1960), 35.

5. Leonard Ravenhill noted, *"The early church was married to poverty, prisons and persecutions. Today, the church is married to prosperity, personality, and popularity."* Leonard Ravenhill, *Why Revival Tarries* (Minneapolis: Bethany House, 2004), 44.

6. Charles Spurgeon warned, *"If your religion does not make you holy, it will damn you. It is simply painted pageantry to go to hell in."* See also: *"An unholy church! It is useless*

to the world, and of no esteem among men. It is an abomination, hell's laughter, heaven's abhorrence. The worst evils which have ever come upon the world have been brought upon her by an unholy church." Charles H. Spurgeon, *Metropolitan Tabernacle Pulpit*, vol. 42 (London: Passmore & Alabaster, 1896), 271.

7. Jesus Himself declared, "No one can serve two masters; for either he will hate the one and love the other, or else he will be loyal to the one and despise the other" (Matt. 6:24 NKJV).

8. The designation "The Way" appears multiple times in Acts (9:2; 19:9, 23; 22:4; 24:14, 22) as the early name for Christianity, emphasizing that following Christ was not merely holding an opinion but walking a singular path of life.

9. Tozer observed, *"The vague and tenuous hope that God is too kind to punish the ungodly has become a deadly opiate for the consciences of millions."* A.W. Tozer, *The Knowledge of the Holy* (New York: Harper & Row, 1961), 87.

10. The "second death" is referenced in Revelation 20:14–15: "Then Death and Hades were cast into the lake of fire. This is the second death. And anyone not found written in the Book of Life was cast into the lake of fire" (NKJV).

11. Ravenhill captured this truth: *"There is one thing we need above everything else; it is something we do not talk about these days. We need a mighty avalanche of conviction of sin."* Leonard Ravenhill, *Revival God's Way* (Minneapolis: Bethany House, 1983), 31.

12. 12. Tozer pleaded, *"I want God to do something new for me—to revive my spirit, to change my dingy gray to white, to make me sick of compromise, weary of this checkered living. Pray for me that I might become a holy man, a holy woman indeed by the blood of the Lamb and the fire of the*

Holy Ghost." A.W. Tozer, *Whatever Happened to Worship?* (Camp Hill, PA: Christian Publications, 1985), 98

Unburdened Preachers

In the year of 2014 the Lord instructed me to read the Gospels with no rush. As I read the first account of Jesus' life, I became stuck on a certain passage: *"Take My yoke upon you, and learn from Me."*[1] I began to camp over those words, reading it every morning and every night. Praying it, talking about it, asking the Father to reveal Himself to me and yoke me with Christ. I asked Him to consume me with the desire of Christ and found myself wanting His words more than my own. I wanted His will more than my own. I wanted to walk like Him and think like Him. As I prepared myself to write this chapter, I heard the Lord ask, *"Preacher, are you yoked with Christ?"*

As the Lord has released this holy confrontation in the Church, there is—and is going to be—an enlightenment upon the pulpit of preachers who preach yoked by the burden of the Lord and those that are not. There are preachers that may believe in the message of the true Gospel yet preach without the burden of the Lord. Preachers that have given themselves and their congregations to comfort and have neglected the burden of the Lord. Who search the Bible for sermons that fit their message and neglect what thus says the Lord. Leonard Ravenhill stated:

The tragedy of this hour is that we have too many dead men giving out dead sermons to dead people. Why? Because the strange thing today which exists in the pulpit is a horrible thing: it is preaching without unction. What is unction? It's hard to define. Preaching without unction kills instead of giving life. The unctionless preacher is a savor of death unto death. The Word does not live unless divine unction is upon the preacher. Preachers, with all thy getting—get unction from above! Preaching is a spiritual business. A sermon born in the head reaches the head, but a sermon born in the heart reaches the heart...Unction is like dynamite—it will pierce, it will sweeten, it will soften. When the hammer of logic and the fire of human zeal fail to open the stony heart, unction will succeed. [2]

There are preachers that may have not blatantly spoken against the Christ of the Bible, yet deny Him access to their pulpits, their platform, their messages. Preachers, as Ravenhill states, without unction, void of power, void of the blessing, void of conviction. Preachers that give themselves to lifeless sermons that sanction slumber. We enter our pews and listen to the lukewarm messages of our lukewarm preachers. Preachers that are yoked to good phrases, yoked to the mission to grow in numbers, yoked to the opinions of their financial donors, yoked to their mentors, even yoked to their prayerless wives and husbands; but they are powerless, lifeless, lukewarm, stoic preachers without being yoked to The Anointed One, Jesus. [3]

The honest truth is that it is all too rare to see a preacher yoked with the Lord. A preacher that has lost the fear of man and carries the weightiness of the fear of the Lord. It is all too rare to hear a sermon birthed from the received burden of the Lord brought forth. Many will rise to defend their compromise against a righteous sermon brought forth by a righteous preacher, but it is too common for us to see the preacher buckle under the pressure of their opposers. It is because they buckle that we know the true yoke they carry.

Elijah, the preacher of God, proclaimed the message of righteousness, called fire down from heaven, humiliated and purged the land of false preachers, and prayed unto the ending of a three-year drought. Who later, by the hand of the Lord being upon him, outran the horses and chariots of the king. This Elijah was now to face his opposer. He was now to be tested; the fire now came to his heart to determine whether he was secured under the yoke of the Lord. Scripture records that a messenger from his opposer was sent to Elijah, saying, *"So let the gods do to me, and more also, if I do not make your life as the life of one of them by tomorrow about this time."*[4] Then he was afraid, and he arose and ran for his life. Elijah, the great preacher, confronted by the authorities of hell, opposed by the human rage of wickedness, was found lacking security under the yoke.

There are preachers like Elijah today—preachers that don't stand for the truth because they are not securely positioned under the yoke of Christ. They fear the opposers; they pursue fads and trends to be accepted. Oh, preachers that when the name of Christ is defamed amongst them sit quietly and compromise the truth. Preachers that are bold amongst their kind yet before the world timid and powerless, loving their own lives more than Christ. Preachers that believe the end purpose of their ministry is to hold a microphone and be a motivational speaker. Preachers that waver by every wind of doctrine, young preachers who have not been grounded in the word of truth to handle it rightly. Preachers given to systems and well-greased machines, yet lack security under the yoke. Not at all burdened by the heart of the Lord unto the surrender of their own lives, wants, and desires.

There were preachers like this other than Elijah, in the account of Samuel. Eli the high priest and his sons, Hophni and Phinehas. These men were priests, anointed and set apart from all men to serve and minister before the Lord. They were sanctioned to behold the glory of the Lord and convey His heart and judgments of mercy and righteousness. Yet they were not secured under the yoke of the Lord. They denied the Lord's righteousness so much so that Scripture called them *"corrupt,"* for *"they did not know the LORD."*[5] Preacher, the test of your worth is if you truly know God. Not know the Scriptures alone, or the Christian language, or know how to preach and excite people. Do you know God? Do you know the Lord? We are guilty of worthless ministries, because we host and welcome worthless preachers into our pulpits that know not God. Unburdened preachers that find peace in their studies as lifeless expositors of Scripture, yet void of any power to heal the sick, raise the dead, cast out devils, or even speak with the authority given by the resting of God's Spirit upon them.

Even Eli the high priest failed to bring correction to his sons, like many mature preachers today. We have turned our face from making sure that the preacher is blessed of God before we allow them in our pulpits. Pastors, have you no care for your congregants? Have you no care for your flock, that you would allow an unburdened, yoke-less preacher to stand before them with a message that rests on the arm of his own flesh? Preachers, are you ordaining so quickly without making sure that he is anointed and he has surrendered his life to the yoke of Christ? Preachers, I warn you, be not careless with the ministry before the Lord. You must be yoked with Christ. You must not forsake the cost of following Him. *"In all thy getting—get an unction."* Forsake the preaching that rests on the arm of your own flesh, your own experience, your own opinions. If you are a preacher and you have not waited for the burden of the Lord to come upon you before you mount the pulpit, may you repent. Repent and turn back, that you may receive the yoke of the Lord, learn from Him and know Him. For many preachers will reach the seat of judgment and God will require of them the fruit of His predestined will, and they will come up empty. Because their ministries were founded on their gifts and their talents in the name of Christ. Prophets that have claimed their position using the function to exploit the people of God and lead them astray. Prophets with amazing demonstrations of gifts, knowing names not by the Lord but by familiar spirits, not by the Lord but in His name, will stand before the Lord and He will examine their necks and shoulders. He will examine them for the imprints of His yoke. He will see if they were bondservants or just mere impersonators. And many of them will depart from Him, because they are missing the imprint, they are missing evidence of the yoke, the burden of the Lord.

In the days of the early Church there was a man called Simon the Sorcerer. This man went around preaching *"that he himself was somebody great."* People gathered around him and were amazed by his magic and even declared, *"This man is the great power of God."*[6] He claimed to have the power of God, until Philip, one that had been truly endued with power from heaven, whom the Holy Spirit rested on, came and preached the gospel of the Kingdom of God and the name of Jesus Christ. The people believed and were baptized, even Simon. And Simon, intrigued by the demonstrations of the Holy Spirit through Philip, followed in amazement.

When the other apostles heard of the good news they sent Peter and John to pray for them that they might receive the same Holy Spirit, to have the same power Philip operated in and be secured under the yoke of Christ. The apostles laid their hands upon the people that they might receive the Holy Spirit and they did! When Simon saw, he ran to his house and found all the money he could and came to the apostles offering an exchange. His silver—for the power of the Holy Spirit, for the gift of God. Peter rebuked the intent of his heart and called him to repent. For power cannot be bought.

Like Simon, today preachers want to follow a certain ministry and submit themselves to certain systems of financial pocketing to somehow buy what only can come from God. Preachers trying to pay one another for the gifts and talents. We have preachers that have prostituted their anointing and gifts that God unrepentantly gave them, now charging a certain fee for their services. Oh, what we have made of the blood of Christ, the true price for the gifts of God.

Scripture states, *"Buy the truth, and do not sell it."*[7] Oh, but we have sold our truth, we have given away our preciousness for the affirmation of men. We have sold ourselves into the slavery of the system for fame and money, for public recognition. In that, God has removed His burden from you; you have rejected the yoke of the Lord and have been fired. Yet you continue to minister in the name of the Lord. I warn you preachers, return to the Lord while His kindness can reach you and His forbearance is abundant. Step not into eternity responsible for the eternal damnation of many. Turn from your corruption and seek the Lord while He can be found. Do not allow the darkness that covers the earth in unprecedented thickness to consume you too. Repent, seek forgiveness and forsake your religious prostitution. Surrender your gifts and talents unto the Lord and stay at His feet until the intents of your hearts are purified. Return to the Cross and forsake your lust for money and public recognition. Save your own souls and fear the Lord and His coming judgment. Return to the wilderness of obscurity until God masters the wildness of your hearts in all its rebellion. Pastors, take care again of your congregants and think it not a business. For you are held responsible to govern the sanctity of the pulpit. Let those that preach, preach Christ and Christ alone!

There was a preacher of God called Jonah. The Lord commanded him to go to a certain place and preach repentance. But he rebelled within his heart against the word of the

Lord. So he ran away from the presence and burden of the Lord. He ran away from the commandment of God into a ship going the total opposite way. In his disobedience God released a storm against his caravan of rebellion. He was thrown into the sea, drowned and swallowed by a fish, as his soul proceeded to hell. While his body rested in the fish's belly, Jonah prayed from the belly of hell for God to rescue him, crying for forgiveness. The Lord spoke to the fish to spew him out upon the land and he was redeemed. The preacher, saved from an eternity in hell, repented of his rebellious ways and was saved. Are you like Jonah? Are you rebelling against the word of the Lord? Do you carry integrity with the word of truth? Or have you allowed your rebellion to deceive your heart to think that obedience is an option? Preacher, run not away from the burden of the Lord; submit your lives and obey. Fear God and submit to His commands. Preach only what He authorizes and condemn all other messages. Preach the name of Jesus Christ. We have taken the burden of the Lord off of our shoulders that we might ignore His sovereignty and His justice. *"Do not be deceived, God is not mocked; for whatever a man sows, that he will also reap."*[8] What will you reap, preacher? What is the cost of mishandling the name and word of the Lord? Will you not pay it, for denying the Lord's anointing in your pulpit? Yes you will, if you do not seek the Lord while He may be found. Cry out to Him while His heart is toward you to answer, to work forth righteousness in your life and complete the good work He started within you, that you have forsaken for too long.

I tell you the truth, God is still the creator of tempests. And if you do not repent, the tempest that is coming upon the earth will swallow you up and instead of redemption, eternity will meet you and finalize your judgment. This is the truth; this is what is to come upon us. For those that are with the Lord will be saved and preserved, but those that are against Him will not be. Fear God. Turn your hearts back to Him and ask His forgiveness. Dedicate your lives and ministries back to Him and re-enter the faith and hope of the coming glory. Offer your neck and shoulders to Him again. Welcome the yoke of the Lord, that you may be baptized by the Spirit of God, that He may come upon you that you may be enabled to preach Christ and Christ alone with power and authority. Return to the burden of the Lord. Seek the burden of the Lord. Learn from Him and know Him. Secure your own souls. Repent, for the Kingdom of God is at hand. He who has an ear to hear, let him hear what the Spirit says.

Endnotes

1. Matthew 11:29 (NKJV): *"Take My yoke upon you and learn from Me, for I am gentle and lowly in heart, and you will find rest for your souls."* The full invitation of Christ in Matthew 11:28–30 calls the weary to find rest not in religion but in relationship, not in performance but in submission to the easy yoke of the Master.

2. Leonard Ravenhill, *Why Revival Tarries* (Minneapolis: Bethany House, 2004), 19–21. Ravenhill further writes: *"Unction cannot be learned, only earned—by prayer. Unction is God's knighthood for the soldier-preacher who has wrestled in prayer and gained the victory."*

3. E.M. Bounds echoes this same burden in *Power Through Prayer* (Grand Rapids: Zondervan, 1991), 40: *"Unction is the one divine enablement by which the preacher accomplishes the peculiar and saving ends of preaching. Without this unction there are no true spiritual results accomplished; the results and forces in preaching do not rise above the results of unsanctified speech."*

4. 1 Kings 19:2 (NKJV). Jezebel's threat came immediately after Elijah's greatest victory on Mount Carmel. The prophet who had faced 450 prophets of Baal and called fire from heaven now fled from the rage of one woman—a sobering reminder that spiritual power without continual abiding under Christ's yoke can quickly give way to fear.

5. 1 Samuel 2:12 (NKJV): *"Now the sons of Eli were corrupt; they did not know the LORD."* The Hebrew term translated "corrupt" (beliya'al) literally means "worthless" or "sons of wickedness." They knew the rituals but not the Lord—a fatal distinction for those entrusted with holy ministry.

6. Acts 8:9–10 (NKJV). Simon the Sorcerer represents all who seek spiritual power for personal gain rather than for the glory of God. His attempt to purchase the Holy Spirit with money reveals a heart that had never truly submitted to the yoke of Christ.

7. Proverbs 23:23 (NKJV): *"Buy the truth, and do not sell it, also wisdom and instruction and understanding."* Truth is to be obtained at any cost but never bartered away for popularity, comfort, or financial gain.

8.   Galatians 6:7 (NKJV). A.W. Tozer warned: *"To be effective, the preacher's message must be alive. It must alarm, arouse, challenge—it must be God's present voice to this particular people."* See A.W. Tozer, *Of God and Men* (Harrisburg, PA: Christian Publications, 1960), 27.

Baggage in the Pulpit

The burdens of the Lord are holy. They are sacred and should be treated as such. The burdens of the Lord demand holiness, sanctification, and a life lived above reproach. Scripture commands preachers to *"be blameless, the husband of one wife, temperate, sober-minded, of good behavior, hospitable, able to teach; not given to wine, not violent, not greedy for money, but gentle, not quarrelsome, not covetous; one who rules his own house well, having his children in submission with all reverence (for if a man does not know how to rule his own house, how will he take care of the church of God?); not a novice, lest being puffed up with pride he fall into the same condemnation as the devil. Moreover he must have a good testimony among those who are outside, lest he fall into reproach and the snare of the devil."*[1] In other words, holiness and righteousness are required.

We have treated the pulpit and handled the word of God with contempt, because we have forsaken such a life. We have made excuses for our sins, even published our sins for all to see in hopes of being "authentic"—when actually it is decaying our witness. Yes, our witness before men in public and before spirits in the unseen. Some of us pose a good look in public and on our social media and before many crowds, but we cannot fool the spirits within the unseen realm that are at all times watching our every move. Scripture declares, *"the devil walks about like a roaring lion, seeking whom he may devour."*[2] The enemy is ever-ready to accuse us of wickedness. For his end purpose is *"to steal, and to kill, and to destroy."*[3] And he has successfully done so with many preachers who are unholy and *"profane...like Esau, who for one morsel of food sold his birthright."*[4]

We have sold our re-birthright of justification and sanctification for moments of sin and pleasure. We sell our birthright every time we click on that website or watch that movie. We sell our birthright when we excuse that curse word or that crude joke. We sell our birthright when we give ourselves one more slice of the pizza that crosses the threshold from full to gluttony. We sell our birthright when we flirt back with the receptionist knowing our wives and families await us at home. There are pastors who have sold their birthright, secretly engaging in perverse acts with other men. Oh, many of us have sold holiness for pleasure and righteousness for a moment of cheap bliss. We sell our birthright when we decide in our hearts to gossip, or lie, or cheat. We sell it and we, *"crucify again...the Son of God, and put Him to an open shame."*[5]

Don't you see what the enemy seeks to do by enticing you to sin? By encouraging you to publish it for all to see in the name of authenticity and grace? He, through you, wills to openly shame Christ. And many of us have. For preachers are in more scandals than dirty car-salesmen. The world, by the agenda of its god, seeks to show us to be as sinful as they are— they seek the homosexual pastor, the money-hungry prophet, the whoring worship leader, and the gossiping first lady. Don't you see the agenda is not just to destroy you, but for you to destroy the witness of Christ in the earth as you subject Him to public shame and abuse? That old serpent desires to expose you and strip you from every article of righteous clothing, exposing you as naked before principalities, authorities, and hosts of wickedness in the heavenly places. The devil desires to see you powerless.

Family, the bottom line is that for us to carry the burden of the Lord we must be holy. We must come out from among the world and live separated lives unto God. As I began to write this book, an intense attack of temptation and enticement of things I don't even deal with came from the enemy, and the Spirit of the Lord rose up in me and began to proclaim loudly within my spirit, "Spiritual contraceptives! Spiritual contraceptives! Spiritual contraceptives! The enemy desires to force these sins into your heart and mind that you cannot conceive, bear, or birth the purpose of God in your life." When I heard this, resistance became easy.[6]

Preachers, the devil desires to do the same. We have been easily stripped of our purpose and power because we have allowed the bellows of enticement to overtake us. We have allowed the enemy to fill us with spiritual birth control to determine what we conceive and produce. Oh yes, he has taken control of many of our wombs—our inner men are trapped. Where the sermons that we preach are infected with the guilt of our private place, so we don't preach holiness and repentance. Our counsel has been breached because we now teach the sinner that sin is okay because of sin in our own lives. The enemy has stripped us from our authority to preach against pornography with conviction because we ourselves enjoy and are imprisoned by its cheap thrills. We have no strength to teach celibacy for the single mother, no power to deliver the teen addict, because the same demons that plague their hearts and minds sleep on our pillow and lay with us nightly—or just every once in a while.

Preachers, we have resorted to atmosphere and certain dynamics and preach self-help motivational messages that are comfortable and void of any substance because we no longer belong to the cross of Christ. Our sinful flesh no longer hangs nailed to a cross, but we live, move, and have our being in it. And instead of the burdens of the Lord, we carry the baggage of our iniquity. Our baggage tells us how far we can go and how much we can say. From our baggage we preach, from our baggage we create songs, from our baggage we proclaim the unbiblical grace. Oh, the enemy has robbed us of purpose and only seeks to load us with the weights of our weakness and fleshly proclivities. Our lusts and appetites are now our gods.

The perilous times are fully upon us, where "...*men will be lovers of themselves, lovers of money, boasters, proud, blasphemers, disobedient to parents, unthankful, unholy, unloving, unforgiving, slanderers, without self-control, brutal, despisers of good, traitors, headstrong, haughty, lovers of pleasure rather than lovers of God, having a form of godliness but denying its power.*"[7] And how surely we have exploited the form of godliness. Scripture even continues and says these, "*evil men and impostors will grow worse and worse, deceiving and being deceived.*"[8] We are hearers of the word of truth alone, deceiving ourselves in thinking we are doers. We are more filled with resolutions for fleshly and earthly development than we are for true spiritual maturity and discipline. We say to ourselves this is my thorn in the flesh but deny the grace to resist its claim on our actions, our minds, and our hearts. As I write, a spirit of repentance overwhelms my own soul. We must cry to the Lord in repentance and surrender to Him our baggage.

There was a preacher by the name of Balaam.[9] He was sanctioned by a man named Balak to preach against the people of Israel. He would go over to the camping soldiers of Israel and curse them and he would receive payment for it. He was a preacher of God, only to be authorized by the Lord, but within his lust he took the house-load of money. The Lord strictly gave him instructions to only speak and do what was commanded. However, persuaded by the money, he saddled his donkey and went to the men that sanctioned him. On his way, the anger of the Lord was kindled and the Angel of the Lord took His stand against him.

As he was riding along, Scripture says, *"...the donkey saw the Angel of the Lord standing in the way with His drawn sword in His hand, and the donkey turned aside out of the way and went into the field."* Balaam struck his donkey forcing it to continue down the path, for he didn't see the Angel of the Lord. When the donkey went back on the path, she saw the Angel again and turning aside she crushed the foot of Balaam against a wall. He struck her again and she got back on the path. And a third time she saw the Angel—the opposition of the Lord against the ways of Balaam—and laid down on the path.

Balaam struck it again in frustration and something amazing happened—God opened the mouth of the donkey! Yes, the donkey reared her head to Balaam and said, *"What have I done to you, that you have struck me these three times?"* And another amazing thing happened—Balaam didn't even miss a beat, he replied sharply, *"Because you have abused me. I wish there were a sword in my hand, for now I would kill you!"* Oh my goodness! Then the donkey replied, *"Am I not your donkey on which you have ridden, ever since I became yours, to this day? Was I ever disposed to do this to you?"* and he replied, "No." An entirely comfortable conversation with a donkey. Then the Lord opened his eyes to see the Angel standing in the way with His sword in His hand. Immediately, he bowed his head and fell flat on his face. The Angel of the Lord told him that his donkey saved his life three times because, *"Behold, I have come out to stand against you, because your way is perverse before Me."*[10]

Like Balaam we are sinners in the hands of an angry God.[11] God stands in our way, with His wrath ready to consume our lives and bring retribution for our wickedness before Him. The Lord stands against us, for we have trampled underfoot the blood of Christ and have claimed that His grace has excused us. He stands against us for we have used His people and manipulated them for money to answer debts. He stands in our way and the donkey we ride is our ministries. No longer blessed of God, it turns aside and we strike it with campaigns and fleshly strategies to get it back on course. It stays for a bit until it sees the near wrath and turns aside again. We rev it up again with more money, with more speakers and lights and a more modern look and it's back on course in our eyes, but it continues to meet the frightful image of an angry God standing in its way. Soon it turns aside again. And the enemy comes to blind us and trick us to think it's his opposition, yet for many it is the anger of God that we have kindled by walking in a perverse way before Him. Oh that we would see again!

Even when we are crushed we try to continue in our perverse way before the Lord. I hear the Lord proclaim again, *"Vengeance is Mine, and recompense; their foot shall slip in due time; for the day of their calamity is at hand, and the things to come hasten upon them."*[12] Preachers, turn to the Lord quickly and without hesitation. Cleanse yourself of your sinful passions and habits. Call on the name of the Lord and cling again to the cross and may your conscience be sprinkled clean. Cleave to the floor, plant your face toward the dust and humble yourselves. Cry out unto the Lord until He answers in mercy that His wrath may relent and He may bless you with forgiveness. Save your own souls and the souls of your family. For the wrath is not coming to you alone, but it is coming to the household you lead. It is coming to your ministry, church, and organization. It is coming to your disciples. Wash your hands clean of these guilts and hear the kindness of God drawing you to repent!

Turn in your baggage to the Lord and take a coal from the altar and put it upon your lips.[13] Cleanse your messages— throw them away, burn them with fire. Forsake the weights of your past and put away the sin that easily assails you. Hear the

Lord in His kindness and return. Repent, for the kingdom of Heaven is at hand. He who has an ear to hear, let him hear what the Spirit says.

Endnotes

1. 1 Timothy 3:2–7 (NKJV). Paul's instructions to Timothy outline the moral and spiritual qualifications required of those who would oversee God's church—standards that remain binding on ministers today.
2. 1 Peter 5:8 (NKJV). Peter's warning employs the imagery of a predatory lion to describe Satan's aggressive pursuit of believers, particularly those in spiritual leadership who represent high-value targets.
3. John 10:10 (NKJV). Christ contrasts His mission of abundant life with the devil's threefold agenda of theft, destruction, and death.
4. Hebrews 12:16 (NKJV). The Greek word translated "profane" (bebēlos) means "accessible to everyone" or "common"—Esau treated his birthright as ordinary rather than sacred.
5. Hebrews 6:6 (NKJV). The writer of Hebrews employs the shocking imagery of re-crucifixion to describe the gravity of apostasy—particularly relevant to those who preach Christ while living in contradiction to His gospel.
6. Leonard Ravenhill, *Why Revival Tarries* (Minneapolis: Bethany House, 2004), 23: "The pastor who is not praying is playing; the people who are not praying are straying. The pulpit can be a shop window to display one's talents; the prayer closet allows no showing off."
7. 2 Timothy 3:1–5 (NKJV). Paul's catalogue of end-times characteristics describes not merely pagans but those "having a form of godliness"—religious people whose lives contradict their profession.
8. 2 Timothy 3:13 (NKJV). The progression "worse and worse, deceiving and being deceived" reveals a downward spiral—the deceiver becomes increasingly self-deceived.

9. Numbers 22:22–35 (NKJV). The Balaam narrative serves as a sobering warning to ministers who, while possessing genuine prophetic gifting, allow covetousness to corrupt their calling.
10. Numbers 22:32 (NKJV). The Hebrew word translated "perverse" (yarat) indicates a path that deviates from God's intended course—Balaam's way was crooked before the Lord.
11. The phrase "sinners in the hands of an angry God" alludes to Jonathan Edwards' famous sermon of the same name, preached at Enfield, Connecticut on July 8, 1741. Edwards preached from Deuteronomy 32:35, declaring: "The reason why they are not fallen already, and do not fall now, is only that God's appointed time is not come."
12. Deuteronomy 32:35 (NKJV). Moses' Song warns Israel that divine judgment, though delayed, is certain—their "foot shall slip" when God's patience reaches its appointed end.
13. Isaiah 6:6–7 (NKJV). Isaiah's commissioning included the cleansing of his lips by a coal from the altar—a picture of the purification required before one can speak for God.

The Lost Groans of Prayer

Brothers and sisters, take these words to heart. The things you have read and will read are of the utmost importance for the coming days. Mark my words, He is coming back for all those who are holy and blameless before Him. He is closer than yesterday and we know not the hour. Hear the words of the Lord and respond in favor of it. I pray you are filled with the Spirit of wisdom and revelation. He who has an ear to hear, let him hear what the Spirit says.

Family, beyond the habits of wickedness and the compromise of lustful passions, the greatest of these is prayerlessness. The greatest abomination of this time is a prayerless preacher. And it is too common. You may be faithful to your spouse, a benevolent ruler of your household, and loyal to preach the Scripture. But preaching is easy, as Ravenhill states: it can become merely a "combination of memory, knowledge, ambition, personality, plus well-lined book shelves, self-confidence and a sense of having arrived."[1] Yet the Lord says, "I know your works. You have the reputation of being alive, but you are dead."[2] The words ring in the heavens above you prayerless preachers, for you succeed in fooling the crowds but the One who sees all cries aloud, "Woe to you...hypocrites! For you are like whitewashed tombs which indeed appear beautiful outwardly, but inside are full of dead men's bones and all uncleanness."[3]

Seven woes rested on them: They taught about the Lord yet their love had grown cold—they didn't enter the kingdom of heaven themselves, nor permitted others. They converted men unto dead religion, making them twice as much people destined for hell than themselves. They taught that covenant to God in the temple or altar was binding, but an oath by money was greater. They taught the law but neglected to practice the most important part—justice, mercy, and faithfulness in the private place before God. They appeared clean and holy but were full of carnality, greed and self-indulgence. They exhibited themselves as holy on account of being tedious keepers of the law, but it was a mask, for they were full of ungodly thoughts and feelings. They boasted of being descendants of the prophets when in fact they were descendants of persecutors and murderers, and the same blood ran through their veins. Seven woes, seven sins counted against them.[4]

You may not be guilty of swindling men out of money, or neglecting the most important things such as justice, mercy and faithfulness. You may not be full of carnality, or greed and self-indulgence. You may not exhibit yourself as holy on account of being scrupulous with keeping the law. But because of prayerlessness you teach about a God you do not know, your love easily has grown cold. Because of prayerlessness you neglect entering the kingdom of heaven and deny access to others. Because of prayerlessness you convert men unto dead religion, making them twice as destined for hell as you are. Without prayer you cannot know God and without knowing Him you cannot enter His rest. Scripture alone "kills, but the Spirit gives life."[5] Through prayerlessness you are not sealed by the guarantee of the salvation we await. A prayerless man is one void of the Spirit that gives life. A prayerless man is a servant of a dead religion.

Even the ministry that brought condemnation was wrought forth through the consistency of prayer and communion with God's Spirit.[6] Who knows, you may be able to go before God, clothed in the robes of righteousness you knitted for yourself, yet the same words destined for the lawless will meet your ear. For without the Spirit of holiness how are you to present yourself before the Lord blameless? You have believed in the gospel of Christ you say and confessed that He is Lord. So surely you will enter into the rest. Yet without the seal we are easily given to false and dead religion, which cannot enter into heaven. Am I saying you must be filled and have relationship with the Holy Spirit to be saved?

Yes, for Scripture clearly states, "Anyone who does not have the Spirit of Christ does not belong to Him."[7] So how can you have the Spirit if you've never asked? And how can you ask if you do not pray? Yes, you did receive salvation by grace through faith as a gift of God. But without the blessed Holy Spirit your walk is empty and your works are in vain. For Jesus commanded His disciples, "...wait for the promise of the Father, which," he said, "you heard from me; for John baptized with water, but you will be baptized with the Holy Spirit not many days from now."[8] They saw the resurrected Son of God and surely believed in Him, what more is there to being sealed for the redemption to come? What more do they need?

The manifest power and ministry of the Holy Spirit. For Jesus emphasized His importance in the Christian walk a second time stating, "you will receive power when the Holy Spirit has come upon you, and you will be my witnesses in Jerusalem and in all Judea and Samaria, and to the end of the earth."[9] For the Christian life is not about believing and living in dead religion. But giving ourselves to the kingdom of God as witnesses to the resurrected King, and how can we be convincing without power? How can we have power without the Holy Spirit? How can you have the Holy Spirit without asking? And how can we ask without prayer?

One thing the Lord has against you preacher, that makes you lack everything worthwhile, is prayerlessness. It is prayerlessness that keeps your congregants blind, lame and deaf. It is prayerlessness that allows sickness to increase in your pews and the demon oppressed to continue in their imprisonment. It is because of prayerlessness that you have yet to preach a burning sermon. It is because of prayerlessness that your sermons are dead, your congregation is dry and timid, and your ministry ineffective within your family or community. It is because of prayerlessness that you lack the fruit of evangelism and unfailing converts. It is because of prayerlessness all sorts of idolatry and immorality runs wild in your pews.

You might say, "Caleb, I pray all the time, yet these things are true." My answer to you is, no one who has earnestly prayed and waited on the manifest power and ministry of the Holy Spirit ever came up from their knees empty.[10] The understanding the prayerless preacher lacks is that as ministers within the New Testament Church, we are purposed to be "ministers of a new covenant, not of the letter but of the Spirit."[11] We are purposed to be ministers—partakers of the Spirit and His ministry in the earth. For the ministry of the New Testament belongs to the Holy Spirit, for "will not the ministry of the Spirit have even more glory?"[12]

Scripture further instructs us how we must continue in the effectiveness of our ministry with the Spirit: "be filled with the Spirit."[13] The better translation of the same verse says, "be continually and daily filled to fullness with the Spirit." How can we be filled without asking? How can we ask without prayer? And another reason our prayers for healing, or deliverance are many times ineffective is caused by the simple fact that, "we do not know what we should pray for as we ought..."[14] We think of ourselves more highly than we ought. We think a dissertation of knowledge of perfect diction in the ears of God will impress Him to move amongst us with power and glory. God cares nothing about our self-righteous intellect. The prayer that God searches for is the inspired prayer. And how can you utter inspired prayers without the breath of God that inspires all things? And how can you have the breath of God without the Spirit, which literally means the living wind or living breath of God? Scripture further says, "but the Spirit Himself makes intercession for us with groanings which cannot be uttered...[and] He who searches the hearts knows what the mind of the Spirit is, because He makes intercession for the saints according to the will of God."[15] Inspired prayer moves past the self-righteous knowledge of men and gets to the inconceivable knowledge of the Spirit that will consume our very souls unto its very depths which can only be expressed in groans.

Humble, broken, desperate groans, are the prayers that release the will of God which is a powerful witness of Christ unto the salvations of family members and your community. It is those kinds of prayers that release power in the hands of elders to anoint and pray over the sick and to see them recover. It is those kinds of prayers that give you strength to bear the true ministry of the New Testament. It is desperate, broken, rawly inspired prayers by the Spirit within that will work forth righteousness in our lives, will wake us up from our dead religion, and bring restoration to our ministerial effectiveness. It is after those prayers and those prayers alone we can stand before God in His presence and cry, "Arise, Oh Lord, and demonstrate your power!" It is after those prayers that you know the demon oppressed are free and his works have been destroyed. It is by those prayers that you know you are in the will of God.

But we have lost groans of prayer. We have lost it and replaced it with human strategy and cunningness. We have lost the desire to pray because of the same transgression found in Satan and Adam: pride. We have lost the groans and replaced them with bulletins and email marketing. Through prayerlessness we have invoked the curse of God upon our lives and our ministries, for Scripture states, "Cursed is the man who trusts in man, and makes flesh his strength, whose heart departs from the Lord."[16] We have lost the groans of prayer for our sleep. Christ has gotten tired of returning to prayerless servants, He has grown wearier of returning just to say, "What! Could you not watch with Me one hour?"[17] We are bored and heavy with sleep and have lost the groans of prayer consequently. Spiritual boredom has robbed us from partnering with the will of God for our lives. Oh, how he longs to hear a praying bride awaiting His return.

Jesus tells us of ten virgins, who took for themselves lamps and went out in the night to meet the bridegroom. Now five were wise and five were foolish. For the ones who were called foolish took their lamps but brought no extra oil with them, but the wise did. And while the bridegroom was delayed, they all slept. At the darkest point of time a cry was heard, 'Behold, the bridegroom is coming; go out to meet him!' Then all those virgins arose and turned on their lamps. The foolish said to the wise, "Give us some oil, for our lights are going out." But the wise replied, No, lest there should not be enough for us and you; go and buy for yourselves. And while they went out to buy, the bridegroom had come, those who were ready went in with him to the wedding; and the door was shut. The foolish virgins came to the door and cried, "Lord, Lord, open to us!" But he replied, "I don't know you."[18]

Many of us today are like the foolish virgins, it is not that we have given ourselves to another and defiled the vein of our purity, but we have failed to be ready and watch in anticipation of His coming. Christ said, "It is not for you to know times or seasons which the Father has put in His own authority."[19] The hour might come tomorrow when we will hear the sound of His servant declaring, "Behold! The bridegroom is coming; go out to meet him!" Will you be ready, will you be equipped with the oil of the Spirit that is only given to those who ask for Him? Will you be found missing while Christ is passing by?

Preachers of America, Christ is passing through the nations. He is visiting your churches and attending your services, listening to your messages, judging the fruit of your ministries and seeing how you have handled the lamps and oil of the Spirit. Have you hidden it under a basket? Have you discarded it by trusting in the arm of the flesh and the strategies of men. Have you fallen asleep? The bridegroom is passing by and you go to turn your lamp on yet it is going out. Are you equipped with the oil of His Spirit? Do you belong to Him? Notice that the ones with the oil were the ones He knew. Preacher, do you belong to Christ? The question is not if you know Him. For we can claim to know Him by our studies and reading. The questions that He will ask within Himself is does He recognize your face? He will ask, "Do I know your voice?" We can say we know Him by listening to the preaching of others but again as Ravenhill says, "Preaching of the type mentioned affects men; prayer affects God. Preaching affects time; prayer affects eternity. The pulpit can be a shop window to display our talents; the closet speaks death to display."[20] God will not know you by your preaching, friend! He will know you by your prayers! He will only know your voice from the closet, not the pulpit. Will God recognize your hello? Will God recognize you when you say Father? Will God recognize you when you praise His name?

Preacher, you may think you are righteous and true in all of your ways, for "there is a way that seems right to a man, But its end is the way of death."[21] One thing the Lord has against you, "You have the reputation of being alive, but you are dead. Wake up, and strengthen what remains and is about to die, for I have not found your works complete in the sight of my God. Remember, then, what you received and heard. Keep it, and repent. If you will not wake up, I will come like a thief, and you will not know at what hour I will come against you."[22] Wake up preacher, you need the oil! Wake up before the bridegroom comes, you need to be filled with the Spirit. Don't you see your lamp is going out! Don't you see your branches are not bearing fruit! Preacher! Wake up! Earnestly pray for the manifest power and ministry of the Holy Spirit.

You have believed, yet you have not waited to be filled with the power from heaven. You have believed yet you do not host the promise of the Father that only comes by prayer. Wake up! Can you not wait for another hour, can you not pray for another day, week, month, year for the Spirit to be poured out upon you and your congregants? If the Christ, God in flesh, did nothing without the Spirit, how prideful are we to think we can complete in the flesh what began in the Spirit. Wake up! Remember the commandments of Christ, repent of your dead works, your dead religion, your dead sermons and dead prayers. Earnestly pray and await for the Lord to pour out His Eternal Spirit upon you! Be not deceived, the constitution of the New Testament Church has not changed, we are still in desperate need of the Holy Spirit, even more so as time wraps up like a wet cloth. Cry out and spare no waking moment, fast and pray for the Spirit to come upon you that you may be watchful and ready when the King appears. He who has an ear to hear, let him hear what the Spirit says.

End Notes

1. This quote captures the essence of what Leonard Raven-hill often warned against: preaching that relies on human ability rather than divine unction. Compare with his statement: "The pulpit can be a shop window to display our talents; the prayer closet allows no showing off." Leonard Ravenhill, *Why Revival Tarries* (Minneapolis: Bethany House, 2004), 25.
2. Revelation 3:1 (NKJV). This was Christ's message to the church in Sardis, a church that had an outward appearance of spiritual life but was spiritually dead.
3. Matthew 23:27 (NKJV). Part of Christ's seven woes pronounced against the scribes and Pharisees who exhibited religious hypocrisy.
4. These seven woes correspond to the condemnations found in Matthew 23:13-32, where Jesus systematically exposes the religious hypocrisy of the scribes and Pharisees. Their external religiosity masked internal spiritual corruption and rebellion against God's truth.
5. 2 Corinthians 3:6 (NKJV). Paul contrasts the old covenant of the letter (the Law) with the new covenant of the Spirit. Without the Spirit's work, even Scripture knowledge can lead to spiritual death rather than life.
6. This refers to 2 Corinthians 3:7-9, where Paul describes how even Moses' ministry under the old covenant, though it brought condemnation, was attended with divine glory because it was wrought through communion with God.
7. Romans 8:9 (NKJV). Paul makes it clear that possession of the Spirit of Christ is the distinguishing mark of true believers. Without the Spirit, one cannot claim to belong to Christ.

8. Acts 1:4-5 (NKJV). Jesus commanded the disciples to wait for the baptism of the Holy Spirit before beginning their ministry, emphasizing that even believing in Christ was insufficient without the empowerment of the Spirit.

9. Acts 1:8 (NKJV). The Holy Spirit's coming brings power for witness and ministry. This power is essential for effective Christian witness in the world.

10. E.M. Bounds expressed similar conviction about the necessity and efficacy of earnest prayer: "The men who have done the most for God in this world have been early on their knees." E.M. Bounds, *Power Through Prayer* (Chicago: Moody Publishers, 1979), 15.

11. 2 Corinthians 3:6 (NKJV). New Testament ministry is fundamentally different from Old Testament ministry—it is characterized by the life-giving work of the Spirit rather than the condemning letter of the law.

12. 2 Corinthians 3:8 (NKJV). Paul argues that if the ministry of condemnation had glory, how much more glorious is the ministry of the Spirit that brings life and righteousness.

13. Ephesians 5:18 (NKJV). The present tense indicates a continuous action—believers are to be continually filled with the Spirit, not just initially at salvation.

14. Romans 8:26 (NKJV). Human weakness in prayer is addressed by the Spirit's intercession, often through groans that cannot be expressed in human language.

15. Romans 8:26-27 (NKJV). The Spirit intercedes for believers according to God's will, even when they don't know how to pray. This intercession often manifests as groans that transcend human expression.

16. Jeremiah 17:5 (NKJV). Trusting in human strength rather than God brings a curse. Prayerlessness is fundamentally an expression of trust in human ability rather than divine power.

17. Matthew 26:40 (NKJV). Jesus' question to His sleeping disciples in Gethsemane reveals His disappointment with their prayerlessness in His hour of greatest need.
18. The parable of the ten virgins from Matthew 25:1-12 (NKJV). The oil represents spiritual preparedness and the indwelling presence of the Holy Spirit, available only to those who earnestly seek Him.
19. Acts 1:7 (NKJV). Jesus reminds the disciples that the timing of His return is in the Father's authority, emphasizing the need for constant readiness rather than speculation about dates.
20. Leonard Ravenhill, *Why Revival Tarries*, 25. Ravenhill consistently emphasized that God knows His people through their prayer lives, not their public ministry. Prayer affects eternity while preaching may only affect time.
21. Proverbs 14:12 (NKJV). Human wisdom and self-righteousness can lead to spiritual death despite appearing right to human judgment.
22. Revelation 3:2-3 (NKJV). Christ's call to the church in Sardis to wake up from spiritual deadness and return to faithful obedience before His unexpected return as a thief.

The Bronze Heavens

Beyond the preachers and our pulpits lacking the potency of prayer, it also results in a prayerless church. Due to this, we are producing a kind of convert that does not know how to pray. Converts that think prayer is an option. Converts that know not the wonders and miracles wrought forth through prayer. The Church today claims prayer as silent meditation and it is to be exercised in the comforts of our personalities. We think today our personal biases and emotions have more authority than the word of the Lord. We have produced a type of Church that watches four hours of television and spends two hours on social media yet neglects the dusty closet, that hasn't seen their knees since the last tragedy. We have a generation of converts that believe they can define which Scripture and disciplines of the faith apply to them, which ones to partake of and the others to disregard. A generation that, "use vain repetitions as the heathen do. For they think that they will be heard for their many words."[1] We know not what it means to, "labor in birth" or "labor fervently...in prayers."[2] We have a people that ignore and are ignorant of the powers and authorities that be, allowed to go unchecked in the heavenly places. We are a people that have chosen to forget the commands of Scripture concerning this discipline of the faith that says, "pray without ceasing", or "watch and pray, lest you enter into temptation."[3]

And because of our prayerlessness as a body, we have created for ourselves bronze Heavens. We have closed the heavens up by our prayerlessness. The spirit of Elijah came with benevolence within his mission and has repented to repeat the same words he once did, "As the Lord God of Israel lives, before whom I stand, there shall not be dew nor rain..."[4] Because of prayerlessness the dew of God's presence and the latter rain has been delayed.

Prayerlessness is the womb of unbelief, for "the fool has said in his heart, 'There is no God.'"[5] We know dead religion and we trust it, we trust our pastors and our preachers. But when it comes to the Lord God, we say in our heart, "There is no God." Oh the grace we deny, oh the beauty we have yet to see. You might say, "I believe there is a God. I am a christian." But do we really believe there is a God? Because our prayerlessness is our answer. You only believe in God when there is tragedy, we only "send" prayers and thoughts when catastrophe overtakes us, Katrina, 9/11, Baltimore bombings, St.Louis Riots, Sandy Hook Elementary School and more. We only believe in Him when it's convenient. Like a fleeting good thought. But when it comes to a daily walk of faith, we are prayerless. He hears our voice not. Our prayerlessness lets us know what our hearts truly believe. For we say in our hearts, *"Who is the Almighty, that we should serve Him? And what profit do we have if we pray to Him?"*[6]

For we have invoked the curse of disobedience, "your heavens which are over your head shall be bronze...The Lord will change the rain of your land to powder and dust."[7] For "there is none who understands; there is none who seeks after God."[8] Our prayerlessness has been a sort of shaking our fists at God. Saying that our ways are beyond His and our thoughts are more effective. We have invoked the curse because prayerlessness is a declaration of self-reliance. For "Cursed is the man who trusts in man and makes flesh his strength, whose heart departs from the Lord."[9] A declaration of independence has been the doom of our home, communities and nation. We have declared war on dependence on God. It goes against the very definition of the justified. Scripture notes, "The just shall live by faith."[10] Not by strategy, nor by sermons, but by faith. Like living check to check, we live sermon to sermon. Many of us rely on community more than we rely on the Lord. But the true just, the true righteous people of the Lord are to say with their hearts, "Some trust in chariots and some in horses, but we trust in the name of the Lord our God!"[11]

Prayerlessness is renouncing God. For a prayerless people is opt to, "sacrifice to demons, not to God, To gods they did not know, To new gods, new arrivals That your fathers did not fear. Of the Rock who begot you, you are unmindful, And have forgotten the God who fathered you."[12] Prayerlessness is the welcome of false religion. And it runs rampant in our pews. As men sit with their family listening to the weekly dead sermon, their hearts and minds are at home before their precious ESPN. Football has replaced God, Sunday lunch and afternoon nap has captured our attention. We are bored by God, bored by His Word, bored because He is not our God. We have heaped for ourselves new gods, television, food and sleep. Oh yes, we have forsaken the one and only true God for entertainment. Friday night movies by Netflix is our god now. Entertainment has robbed us from the closet and held us hostage, distracted and comfortable, lest we call on the name of the Lord and invoke His mercy. For some of us, its family dinners, or the mall, or our friends that have become the new gods in our lives.

Prayerlessness is an incubator of temptation. Jesus on the night He was to be betrayed brought His best of friends to pray with Him. He said to them, "Sit here while I go and pray over there." As He walked about His disciples watched Him. As He bowed His knee their eyes slowly faded to the sides and eventually down. Their bodies were tired, their hearts sad, their stomachs full. They were comfortable on the tree they leaned on and sleep fell heavy upon their shoulders. Jesus returns to see them asleep and says, "Watch and pray, lest you enter into temptation."[13] It is because of their prayerlessness, that they have yielded to temptations. Brother, it is not because you are pre-sexually-orientated that you are lured by those kinds of temptations, it is because you are prayerless. Seductive spirits have freely walked into our homes and taken our children's innocence because of prayerlessness. Pornography claims thousands of Christian homes not because we fail to teach purity or want it. But we are prayerless. Our closets are filled with coats and shoes and no altar has been built or maintained. The presence of the Lord has departed and the god of this world has entered. That old serpent lives with you because of your prayerlessness. He tells you the fruit is sweet and good and because you do not turn to God you eat the fruit time and time again.

Prayerlessness is the attorney for divorce. It is because of our prayerlessness that the sanctity of marriage has been forsaken. Scripture says, " Husbands, likewise, dwell with them with understanding, giving honor to the wife...as being heirs together of the grace of life, that your prayers may not be hindered."[14] But our prayers are hindered. Because grace doesn't rain without prayer. Understanding and wisdom isn't given to the prayerless. You must ask. Prayerlessness is the cause of ignorance, dishonor, graceless living unto divorce.

Family, the misfortunes and defeats of the Church today are only the harvest of our prayerlessness. We are spiritually robbed and poor. For "you lust and do not have...you fight and war. Yet you do not have because you do not ask."[15] The heavens which are over our heads are like bronze and "the earth which is under you shall be iron."[16] We are robbed of true prosperity and covenant wealth because we are prayerless. The works of our hands are barren because we are barren. Fruitless, because only those who abide in the vine and the vine in Him can bear fruit. He clearly spoke, "As the branch cannot bear fruit of itself, unless it abides in the vine, neither can you, unless you abide in Me."[17]

The enemy is not solely to blame. Our empty altars are the produce of our empty closets. Empty youth ministries are yet another manifestation of prayerless parents. We sing more than we pray. Our songs aren't even praises or worship anymore. They are self-centric declarations of who we now are. Our worship, if we can call it that, no longer mirrors heaven, for they worship and sing to the Lamb, we sing to ourselves most of the time. So we can see, we don't worship and we don't pray.

We must choose between our preference and His power. We cannot have a convenient Christianity and a powerful witness at the same time. Men gave their lives and counted it worthless for the gospel. Paul, the apostle who we have turned into the poster boy of Christianity bravely stated, "what things were gain to me, these I have counted loss for Christ." We can't have our own selfish gain and have Christ. We must choose. We must choose football or Christ, pornography or Christ, comfort or Christ.

As Jesus walked along preaching the gospel and healing the sick, there came a young man with fine robes and servants. He came to Jesus not as unto God but unto a mere teacher saying, "Good Teacher, what good thing shall I do that I may have eternal life?" The answer he expected rested upon his own deed. "what good thing shall I do." He was positioning himself to continue in deeds for what only can be received by grace through faith. He even positioned the Christ by his approach calling Him "Good Teacher." The fallacy of his language is that he is coming to a "good teacher" for something only a God can provide. Jesus acknowledges this, "Why do you call

Me good? No one is good but One, that is, God." Jesus says to continue in good deeds and withholding from the ways of the world but that wasn't the answer. And the young man in robes fashioned for comfort knowingly replied, "All these things I have kept from my youth. What do I still lack?" Jesus answered, "If you want to be perfect, go, sell what you have and give to the poor...and come, follow Me."[18] What a blow to the heart the young man experienced. His deeds were great before men yet the security of his eternity was faulty. He walked away from the Lord with great sorrow because the Good Teacher has requested something only a God can. The Lord demanded obedience and sacrifice, teachers give instruction and training, they don't require one's life. The young man came to meet a mere famous "Good Teacher" void of any intent of sacrificing everything. More so, he desired affirmation in all he had and did. But the Lord piercing the heart demands his life and livelihood for the inheritance of true life. For "everyone who has left houses or brothers or sisters or father or mother or wife or children or lands, for My name's sake, shall receive a hundredfold, and inherit eternal life."[19] The grace he sought was cheap, but the grace he found cost his life.

Yet it is true today in our own lives. We desire to possess the grace only given to those who will surrender their lives. There are many religions with mere good teachers that require complete submission as gods unto the promise of eternal life. But the only one and the only way unto eternal life is to surrender to the Christ and Lord of the Bible. Christ is not just a Savior, He is also Lord. What makes a man saved is not believing in a Savior, it is submitting to a Lord. Scripture demands submission, "if you confess with your mouth the Lord Jesus."[20] Not confess in a resurrected Savior alone, but confess Him Lord, your Master. But the fact is we have made our opinion lord, our preferences and possessions our lords. We have made television and sleep our lords, at every beckon we serve them and at every offense we defend them. Yet we go to the manor of Christ and placate to Him as Lord, thinking eternal life will be the wages of our confession alone and not our evidence. Oh what a fallacy.

We must chose Christ or the other. The bride waiting for the groom anxiously noticed that he has gone missing. She cries out to her sisters to find him saying, "O daughters of Jerusalem, if you find my beloved, than you tell him I am lovesick!" Her sisters reply, "What is your beloved more than another beloved?"[21] That is the answer we must answer, with the sacrifice of our lives. The world scoffs in our faces demanding an answer. "Who is Jesus Christ more than Muhammad, Buddha, or Confucius?" We have tried to argue and be intelligent. But the only worthy answer is the sacrifice of our lives. Christ must be Lord. They must see Christ as Lord before Savior. Only a Lord can save.

Not only must we offer and display sacrificed lives, but the gospel is not to be void of confirmation. Seeing a sacrificed life to the Master, the world will ask, "How can you believe such a thing?" They will and have demanded for sure evidence. How can they believe and pray to a person they believe is dead? We must call on the Lord to, "bear witness both with signs and wonders, with various miracles, and gifts of the Holy Spirit, according to His own will."[22] That's how they knew and were convinced when Christ walked on the earth and that is how they will believe today. But how do we go from prayerless to powerful?

We must awaken the furnace of intercession. Redeem and establish our Cinderella. The words of Ravenhill ring true, "The Cinderella of the Church today is the prayer meeting."[23] " If My people who are called by My name will humble themselves, and pray and seek My face..."[24] is not a command it is an invitation. The trumpets are sounding all around you. Family! The Lord is extending the invitation again! Calling us to awaken the furnace and burn in intercession. To turn the lights on in our closet and lay prostrate before Him. To "cry aloud, spare not" Again declare to the Lord, "Your kingdom come. Your will be done. On earth as it is in heaven." We must discover again the force of prayer.

Family, we must repent for our prayerlessness. Do not simply say sorry. It is no longer time for a simple sorry. It is time to turn our hearts to the Lord and stretch out for the hand of God's power to touch our lives, our witness and our nation again. Spare nothing, be silent no more. Give yourself to beckoning the Lord until He comes and makes Himself known to you. Repent, For the Kingdom of God is at hand. He who has an ear to hear, let him hear what the Spirit says.

Endnotes

1. Matthew 6:7 (NKJV). Christ's warning against meaningless, repetitive prayers that pagans use, thinking they will be heard because of their many words rather than sincere heart communication with God.

2. References to "labor in birth" come from Galatians 4:19 and "labor fervently in prayers" from Colossians 4:12 (NKJV). Both indicate the intense, Spirit-directed intercession that characterizes mature Christian prayer life.

3. 1 Thessalonians 5:17 and Matthew 26:41 (NKJV). These commands emphasize the continuous nature of prayer and its necessity for spiritual watchfulness against temptation.

4. 1 Kings 17:1 (NKJV). Elijah's declaration of drought as divine judgment. The author suggests that modern prayerlessness has similarly closed the heavens to God's presence and blessing.

5. Psalm 14:1 (NKJV). The practical atheism that manifests not in intellectual denial but in living as though God doesn't exist or matter, evidenced by prayerlessness.

6. Job 21:15 (NKJV). The attitude of those who see no practical benefit in serving God or praying to Him, reflecting the heart's true condition regarding divine authority.

7. Deuteronomy 28:23 (NKJV). Part of the covenant curses for disobedience, where the heavens become like bronze—hard, impenetrable, yielding no blessing or divine response.

8. Romans 3:11 (NKJV). Paul's indictment of universal human corruption, showing that apart from grace, none naturally seek God through prayer or worship.

9. Jeremiah 17:5 (NKJV). The curse that comes upon those who trust in human strength and wisdom rather than dependence on God through prayer.

10. Romans 1:17 and Habakkuk 2:4 (NKJV). The foundational principle that the righteous live by faith, not by human strategy or self-reliance.
11. Psalm 20:7 (NKJV). David's declaration of trust in God's name rather than in military might or human resources.
12. Deuteronomy 32:17-18 (NKJV). Moses' song describing Israel's apostasy—how they forgot God and turned to false gods, paralleling modern idolatry through entertainment and material comfort.
13. Matthew 26:40-41 (NKJV). Jesus' command to the disciples in Gethsemane, establishing the connection between prayerlessness and susceptibility to temptation.
14. 1 Peter 3:7 (NKJV). Peter's instruction that demonstrates how prayerlessness disrupts not only divine relationship but human relationships, particularly in marriage.
15. James 4:2 (NKJV). James explains that spiritual poverty and defeat come from failing to ask God in prayer for what He desires to give.
16. Deuteronomy 28:23 (NKJV). The complete curse description—bronze heavens above and iron earth beneath—indicating total spiritual barrenness and unfruitfulness.
17. John 15:4 (NKJV). Jesus' teaching on the vine and branches, showing that apart from abiding connection through prayer, no spiritual fruit is possible.
18. Matthew 19:16-22 (NKJV). The account of the rich young ruler who sought eternal life through good works but was unwilling to surrender his possessions and follow Christ.
19. Matthew 19:29 (NKJV). Jesus' promise to those who sacrifice everything for His sake, contrasting with the rich young ruler's unwillingness to do so.
20. Romans 10:9 (NKJV). The confession required for salvation explicitly names Jesus as Lord, not merely Savior, indicating the necessity of submission to His authority.

21. Song of Solomon 5:8-9 (NKJV). The bride's lovesickness and the challenging question about what makes her beloved superior to others—a question the church must answer through sacrificial living.
22. Hebrews 2:4 (NKJV). God's confirmation of the gospel message through supernatural signs, wonders, and gifts of the Holy Spirit as evidence of its truth.
23. Leonard Ravenhill frequently observed that the prayer meeting had become the neglected "Cinderella" of modern church life, despite being the powerhouse of authentic spiritual revival. Leonard Ravenhill, *Why Revival Tarries* (Minneapolis: Bethany House, 2004), 18.
24. 2 Chronicles 7:14 (NKJV). God's promise of healing and restoration to His people when they humble themselves, pray, seek His face, and turn from their wicked ways.

CALEB J. BREEDLOVE

Fervor Yet No Fire

Hear the word of the Lord to you preachers, "I know your works, that you are neither cold nor hot. I could wish you were cold or hot. So then, because you are lukewarm, and neither cold nor hot, I will vomit you out of My mouth. Because you say, 'I am rich, have become wealthy, and have need of nothing'—and do not know that you are wretched, miserable, poor, blind, and naked."[1]

Preachers today, boast in our wealth, we boast in our ministries, we boast that our style of preaching is widely received and in of ourselves lacking nothing. We boast in their leadership team and staff. We boast in our food pantry for the community, and in the buildings we establish, how many chairs we can fit in the room and fill. We boast in the compliments of the weak and unlearned congregation that is left wanting yet feeling good and excited. We boast that our tithes and offering collection is doubling and that we have no deficit or debt. But in reality we are wretched, pitiable, poor, blind and naked. In reality our works before the Lord stand worthless and empty, because we have fallen from the grace the same way the devil did. Our pride speaks volumes of our god. Not of the Christ but the god of the world. Our pride has stripped us from any virtue, we are destined for misery, we are actually poor even with the millions in our bank account, we are blind of this and naked before the true God.

We may look successful and have passion and a line up of sermons that we can't even shake a stick at, but we are in desperate condition. For in all of our passion and fervor, in all of our dynamic preaching, our soul is left insufficient, our works egocentric and fruitless. Because in the eyes of God we aren't completely surrendered. We have not given ourselves to you. Our love is neither fiery or freezing. We sway between the flesh and try to prostitute the Holy Spirit in hopes of a million dollar offering. We give ourselves to gimmicks and tricks, yet preach as if we were upon our faces before God but in actuality we have only given ourselves to the internet to find someone worth imitating. We have exchanged the way that is right to the Lord for bow-ties and trendy hairstyles. We have sold ourselves to preaching messages not from the throne but from the internet, from someone else's ministry. We neither bear the fruits of the Spirit nor do we claim the works of the flesh. But before God we stand "wretched, miserable, poor, blind, and naked."

You may say, "No Caleb, I love God and He loves me. Therefore I am successful." Do we really love God? Can we truly say we love Him? Jesus declared, "If you love Me, keep, My commandments."[2] For the entirety of man's life is to, "Fear God and keep His commandments, for this is man's all."[3] But we neither fear Him or love Him.

The matter is not the love of God for us. It has been expressed in fullness through the Cross. The love of God for us is full and abounding. The issue we face in our lives today is our love for Him. And what we have done is preach and proclaim the love of God, to be a smoke screen to our lukewarm hearts. Oh yes, We declare, "The love of God is all that matters!" "You must know that God loves you!" and my favorite, "You can't love yourself or anyone else, until you know how much God loves you!" But the issue with knowing the love of God is that it is concealed in the true revelation of the Cross of Christ, which many of our sermons are void of. Scripture says, "Greater love has no one than this, than to lay down one's life for his friends."[4] Also, "But God demonstrates His own love toward us, in that while we were still sinners, Christ died for us."[5] The greatest revelation of the love of God is hidden in an authentic revelation of the cross. We dynamically preach, "God is love." And to us, that's all He is. This God who is love, to us He is void of holiness and demands nothing of us. Like the christ we ourselves created. But this is our own cunning way of slipping through the daunting words of Christ which says, "He who does not love Me does not keep My word."[6]

Lukewarmness is not a life void of lip-service. We say we love Him, yet our works are dead before Him. That is being lukewarm. That is what the Lord detests, a people that say they love him not even knowing or obeying His words. There is more biblical illiteracy than we can even fathom. We pride ourselves in not knowing the Bible, yet we say we love Him. How is that possible? How are we to love Him if we do not know His words? We proudly proclaim, "I don't know my bible like I should..but I know God loves me and that's all that matters." No, that's not all that matters. Our eternity doesn't depend on His love for us, more than our love for Him. He is not going to judge us according to His love. It has already shown and proved through the Cross. We will stand before the Lord and He will judge according to the expression and labor of our love. Am I requiring a work-oriented Christianity? No, I am only expressing again what the Lord spoke to His disciples, "If anyone loves Me, he will keep My word; and My Father will love him, and We will come to him and make Our home with him."[7] I am stating the simple notion that the love we have is incomplete. We are lukewarm because we say we love Him but continue in the ways of the world. We say we love Him, and we glory in His love for us, yet avoid the required labor of love. We boast in our love for Him and His love for us, but in reality we are wretched, destined for misery, found lacking before God, blind to the truth and naked.

The wrath of God is not coming to sons of the devil because of only their actions. God searches the intents of the heart and He knows that our actions, our works are the produce of our love. Scripture says, " this is the condemnation, that the light has come into the world, and men loved darkness rather than light, because their deeds were evil."[8] If anything, we have shown God we don't love Him. We love our gifts, talents, we love the style of preaching we have created. We love our ministries, we love how many seats we fill, we even love money we are getting through simply asking. We love our influence, our platforms and our public image, we love the crowds, and the stage background, we love the music, the lights, we must definitely love the recognition. But we don't love God. We say it, because it is the language of the religion we claim. But in our works we have told God loud and clear that, "We do not love You." We love our pornographic cheap thrills, we love fortune, we even love our one-hour quiet time and our devotional. But the sad fact is the we are blind and cannot see that we simply and most truly don't love Him.

In the days of Samuel, the people of God demanded to be like the other nations. They demanded to be trendy and up to speed with the rest of the world. They demanded a new stage background be set and that the lights be changed. They demanded a king. They said to Samuel, "...make us a king to judge us like all the nations." Samuel deeply grieved prayed and the Lord spoke to him saying, "Heed the voice of the people in all that they say to you; for they have not rejected you, but they have rejected Me, that I should not reign over them."[9] And as I see pastors and preachers making of themselves kings I pray like Samuel, deeply grieved in my own spirit. And the Lord speaks those same words. We are simply rejecting God and His will. We no longer cry, "Your will be done." He now hears the disgusting echo of, "This is what I'm doing to make You relevant and relatable, bless it." We act as if we are doing God a favor in all of this. Because we are set in the way of love but in reality we are wretched, destined for misery, found lacking before God, blind to the truth and naked.

Preachers, God is not searching for fervent preaching. He is search for a fiery heart. We have fervor yet no fire. Of the ten virgins, the five foolish ones were not lacking in fervor. They confessed their love for the bridegroom, like the wise. What they lacked was fueled fire. In our pulpit we don't lack in our fervor or zeal. We lack in fire. The lamp of our love is going out. Our fire is dwindling, our lamps are neither hot or cold. But they are lukewarm. They are just at the point of death. We are just at the point of descending in darkness and groveling for the light of others.

Hear the counsel of the Lord, "buy from Me gold refined in the fire, that you may be rich; and white garments, that you may be clothed, that the shame of your nakedness may not be revealed; and anoint your eyes with eye salve, that you may see."[10] Come and buy from Him. Buy from the Lord gold because its will make your work rich, "For we are God's fellow workers; you are God's field, you are God's building…now if anyone builds on this foundation with gold, silver, precious stones, wood, hay, straw, each one's work will become clear…because it will be revealed by fire; and the fire will test each one's work, of what sort it is."[11]

Many of us through our fleshly zeal have forsaken gold, silver and precious stones. We build our ministries with wood, hay and straw. We have exchanged what is valuable for what is burnable. If we have no fire now, there is a fire that awaits to test the labor of love. And what will that fire tell of your labor? May it not be so that you perish with the fire that purges your works.

Buy from the Lord garments of pure white to cover you na-kedness. To cover your shame, to end the reign of guilt. May your heart delight in the the Lord alone and cry, "I will greatly rejoice in the Lord, My soul shall be joyful in my God; for He has clothed me with the garments of salvation, He has covered me with the robe of righteousness."[12] Buy from the Lord oint-ment for the blindness of your eyes. Request of Him to grant you, "the Spirit of wisdom and revelation in the knowledge of Him, the eyes of your understanding being enlightened."[13]

You may say, "How? How can I buy from the Lord?" The Lord answers, "you who have no money, Come, buy and eat. Yes, come, buy wine and milk Without money and without price. Why do you spend money...your wages for what does not satisfy?...Seek the Lord while He may be found, Call upon Him while He is near. Let the wicked forsake his way, And the unrighteous man his thoughts; Let him return to the Lord, And He will have mercy on him."[14]

Preachers, deceive yourselves no more. Give yourself to the greatest commandment again, "...love the Lord your God with all your heart, with all your soul, and with all your mind."[15] For He says to you, "As many as I love, I rebuke and chasten. Therefore be zealous and repent."[16] His love is ever before you. Repent of lukewarmness, forsake such labor. He who has an ear, let him hear what the Spirit says.

Endnotes

1. Revelation 3:15-17 (NKJV). Christ's message to the church in Laodicea, condemning their lukewarm condition despite their material wealth and perceived spiritual success.
2. John 14:15 (NKJV). Jesus establishes obedience to His commandments as the fundamental test and evidence of genuine love for Him.
3. Ecclesiastes 12:13 (NKJV). Solomon's conclusion that the fear of God and keeping His commandments constitute the whole duty and purpose of human existence.
4. John 15:13 (NKJV). Jesus' definition of the greatest love—the laying down of one's life for friends—which He demonstrated on the cross.
5. Romans 5:8 (NKJV). Paul's declaration of how God demonstrated His love through Christ's death while we were still sinners and enemies.
6. John 14:24 (NKJV). Jesus' statement that those who don't love Him are evidenced by their failure to keep His word, exposing the true condition of the heart.
7. John 14:23 (NKJV). Jesus' promise that genuine love for Him will result in obedience to His word and the Father's reciprocal love and presence.
8. John 3:19 (NKJV). The basis of divine condemnation—not ignorance, but the deliberate choice to love darkness rather than light because of evil deeds.
9. 1 Samuel 8:5-7 (NKJV). Israel's demand for a king like other nations, which God interpreted not as rejection of Samuel but as rejection of divine kingship itself.
10. Revelation 3:18 (NKJV). Christ's counsel to the lukewarm Laodicean church to buy from Him gold refined by fire, white garments, and eye salve to address their spiritual poverty, nakedness, and blindness.

11. 1 Corinthians 3:9-13 (NKJV). Paul's teaching about building on the foundation of Christ with materials that will either survive or be consumed by the testing fire of divine judgment.
12. Isaiah 61:10 (NKJV). The prophet's expression of joy in salvation, being clothed with garments of salvation and the robe of righteousness.
13. Ephesians 1:17-18 (NKJV). Paul's prayer for believers to receive the Spirit of wisdom and revelation leading to enlightened understanding of God's calling and inheritance.
14. Isaiah 55:1-7 (NKJV). God's invitation to come and receive spiritual nourishment without money, coupled with the call to seek the Lord while He may be found and return to Him for mercy.
15. Matthew 22:37 (NKJV). Jesus' declaration of the greatest commandment—to love God with all one's heart, soul, and mind.
16. Revelation 3:19 (NKJV). Christ's explanation that His rebuke and chastening of the lukewarm church springs from His love, coupled with the call to be zealous and repent.

The Calling and Commitment

Preacher, hear the word of the Lord, "Is this the ministry I've chosen for you? Or have you chosen it because it was profitable and noble?" I write with a heavy heart. For I write to warn of the two dangers facing the pulpit today. A calling without a commitment and a commitment without a calling. Let's deal with the first one: A commitment without a calling.

Family, so many of our preachers are in danger. They recline unknowingly at the picnic table of God's wrath. Many of the preachers that we follow are in two predicaments. The first predicament is that they committed to a role without being called. We have preachers that are preachers for profit, or preachers because their parents made them to be. We even have preachers that are preachers because of their communications skills. But the anger of God is stirred against you preachers for God isn't too kind on those who hinder His called. You are holding the platform, you are only an empty shell and a barrier. You have committed to a role you've never been called to be in.

King Uzziah, was an anointed ruler of Israel. The Lord found great pleasure in His deeds, for he walked righteously before the Lord and did what was good. His fame spread throughout all the land. However, when he became strong, his heart became pride, "to his destruction, for he transgressed against the Lord his God by entering the temple of the Lord." A person anointed to be king was to enter the throne room, the court-room, the scribes' quarters, but because of his pride he crossed the line and into a danger zone. He went somewhere he was never called to be. He entered the temple of God which only the priest, who were the only ones sanctioned and called to keep. He went, "to burn incense on the altar of incense."[1] What would possess a man to do something that he knew would stir the anger of the Lord? Oh great a sin it is to stir the anger of the Lord. When he was corrected by the priest the Lord gave him a chance to repent and turn back. But his pride bound him and he became furious as he held the incense in his hands. Suddenly, "leprosy broke out on his forehead...because the Lord had struck him."[2] The Lord responded in His holiness and anger and struck Uzziah with leprosy unto death. Am I saying a bunch of preachers are gonna break out in leprosy? Who knows if the judgment of God will be released in the flesh for all to see. But I don't know that there is a judgment that awaits a preacher lacking the commission of the Lord.

The second predicament, is the preacher whose license has been revoked by the Lord yet continues to work. Saul, chosen by the people against the Lord was marked to be the king of Israel. The Lord in His benevolence rested upon him to lead and guide him in the ways of His heart. The anointing would only rest on Saul if he continued in the ways of God. But he didn't and so the Lord lifted His anointing and fired Saul. Yet Saul continued to be king. The Lord even spoke to him through Samuel saying, "Now your kingdom shall not continue" and, "The Lord has sought for Himself a man after His own heart, and the Lord has commanded him to be commander over His people, because you have not kept what the Lord commanded you."[3] You have been cut off and replaced. Yet Saul continued to reign and defy God. Even when the anointing has lifted and the will of God was set against His throne, he continued to go against the Lord in utter disobedience. To the point where God came to Samuel, His friend and said, "I greatly regret that I have set up Saul as king, for he has turned back from following Me, and has not performed My commandments."[4]

How many preachers do we have today that you think God laments over? Do you know for a fact that you are one of those preachers? Pastor, have you been ordained by God or by your friend? Have you been brought into being a servant by the Lord or by the generations before. It is a dangerous thing to involve yourself in something you've never been called to. The calling of God doesn't take place by blood, it is imparted by the word of the Lord touching your ears. Churches are dying because you have been fired yet you continue to work and your judgment is set according to the principles of God lest you repent. There are many of us that are evangelists, pastors and teachers in the Church when we are only meant to be choir members. Just because your father was a pastor doesn't mean the same calling is on our life. And just because you prophesied that one time doesn't establish you as a prophet. I heard a person say to me, "I think we are going to be surprised at the mercy of God on the day of judgment." But as I continue to study the word and pray accordingly, I am grieved to notice that the surprise will not be in His mercy or forbearance with us. We will be surprised what and who He pours His wrath upon.

Preacher, you were once a prophet of the Lord, but because you treated His word carelessly you have been fired. Preacher, you were once sent, but because you now lead men to the wide path you have been cut off. Preacher, you are only famous and seemingly because of the blessing of the people not of the Lord. You are "churched" but not called, and when you cross the threshold of eternity your soul will be revealed to have no part in God, thus you will be hindered from entering His rest. My heart races as the fear of the Lord is so potent in these words. Take it not lightly. If you are not meant to be and you know it when your heart, turn to the Lord in repent. Know that the system you've sold yourself to is deceitful, it is possible to obey the Lord. If you were never called, repent and do not continue. Save your own soul.

Then there is the second danger: one called yet not committed. May the fear of the Lord descend upon you. How dare you ignore the word of the Lord concerning your life. We have given our free will two much authority. Christ says, "All authority in heaven and on earth has been given to me."[5] All authority in heaven and earth is Christ's, meaning that our free will do not deserve any as we stand before our risen Lord. When you enlisted in this army you lost the right to say No. The only word worthy to the utter before the Lord is simply—yes. Salvation is only if Christ is your Lord. Until He is Master of our entire being, and has tamed the wild will of your soul, your salvation is incomplete. Scripture states, "work out your own salvation with fear and trembling."[6] Oh what fear and trembling is there for a person that have not heeded the call of God. Jonah ran away from God. Think about Moses who ran away from his purpose in Egypt. Elijah ran away from the completion of His person. One met God's wrath, the second an encounter of holiness and the last was replaced. One of those results belonged to you friend. For, "Do not think in your heart that you will escape...for if you remain completely silent at this time, relief and deliverance will arise...from another place, but you...will perish."[7] It is a fearful ordeal to reach heaven and God requires of you the fruits of the labor you did not bear. "There is a way that seems right to a man, but its end is the way of death."[8]

There was a man going on a journey. Before he left he chose from amongst his house three servants. To one he gave five talents, to another he gave two, and to the last he gave the last, each according to their ability. The one with the five talents doubled it, the one the two double his as well. But the one with one dug it the ground and hid it. His master came back and congratulated two for double that which he had given them saying, "Well done, good and faithful servant. You have been faithful over a little; I will set you over much. Enter into the joy of your master." But to the one who return the assignment without producing anything the master answered, "You wicked and slothful servant!...cast the worthless servant into the outer darkness. In that place there will be weeping and gnashing of teeth." Jesus states, "No one, when he has lit a lamp, puts it in a secret place or under a basket."[9]

What will you hear when you get to heaven? What will He speak to you? Will the Master say, "Well done good and faithful!" Or will he reply to your excuses of disobedience, "You wicked and slothful servant!" If you are called to preach, preach. If sing, sing. If prophesy, prophesy. If give, give. Let everyone do what the Lord has called for them to. For it is written, "obedience is better than sacrifice."[10] Do not show up on that Day empty-handed and lacking the fruit that He has require of you. He is your Father and He does love you. But His love doesn't make Him less Sovereign. Repent, for the kingdom of God is at hand. He who has an ear, let him hear what the Spirit says.

Endnotes

1. 2 Chronicles 26:16 (NKJV). King Uzziah's transgression when he pridefully entered the temple to burn incense, a function reserved exclusively for the priests.
2. 2 Chronicles 26:19-20 (NKJV). The Lord's immediate judgment upon Uzziah when he refused correction—leprosy breaking out on his forehead as divine punishment for usurping priestly authority.
3. 1 Samuel 13:13-14 (NKJV). Samuel's declaration to Saul that his kingdom would not continue because of

disobedience, and that God had sought a man after His own heart to replace him.

4. 1 Samuel 15:11 (NKJV). God's expression of regret over making Saul king because of his continued rebellion and failure to perform God's commandments.

5. Matthew 28:18 (NKJV). Christ's declaration that all authority in heaven and earth has been given to Him, establishing His absolute sovereignty over all human will and decision.

6. Philippians 2:12 (NKJV). Paul's instruction to work out salvation with fear and trembling, emphasizing the serious responsibility of responding to God's calling.

7. Esther 4:13-14 (NKJV). Mordecai's warning to Esther that if she remains silent in her hour of calling, deliverance will arise from another source, but she and her family will perish.

8. Proverbs 14:12 (NKJV). The warning that what seems right to human understanding may actually lead to spiritual death and destruction.

9. Matthew 25:14-30 and Luke 11:33 (NKJV). The parable of the talents demonstrates accountability for using God-given abilities, while the lamp passage shows that calling is meant to be visible and fruitful, not hidden.

10. 1 Samuel 15:22 (NKJV). Samuel's declaration that obedience to God's calling is better than religious sacrifice, emphasizing the priority of responding to divine commission over ritualistic service.

The Hour of Repentance

Then how are we to respond? "Now, therefore," says the Lord, "Turn to Me with all your heart, With fasting, with weeping, and with mourning." So rend your heart, and not your garments; Return to the Lord your God, For He is gracious and merciful, Slow to anger, and of great kindness; And He relents from doing harm. Who knows if He will turn and relent, And leave a blessing behind Him..."[1] Mourning is the most painful, horrific process of the human soul, yet the most rewarding in the Christian life. Mourning has always been the effect of something or someone valuable dying. We mourn our cats and dogs when they pass away. We mourn for our love ones, which makes a bit more sense to me. But one thing that you seldom witness is a man in total anguish of heart over his sins. A man or woman alike totally undone by the fruit of the flesh and the condition of the spirit.

There was a man and woman that was planted in a garden dedicated to intimate proximity with God. The Garden of Eden was a place of unlimited access to the Father and to His glory— the weight and closeness of His very essence. Where there is glory there is an order, a code of conduct is there not just to limit man but to maintain the man's heart toward the Lord. Glory follows order. God said to the man, "This is my only code of conduct in my garden, you can eat of every tree but not of the tree of good and evil." One code, one law you may say, that was deemed the only thing necessary to maintain the glory of God. Oh, what presence we would be living in, what paradise to not have to deal with rebuke, or reconciliation but be in perfect harmony and community with God. The offense of that one law had one consequence: death. Death in spirit, by the futility of the mind and the end of free correspondence with God. Oh how greatly bitter was that death. It is speculated that the woman and man cut off from God with a hidden promised of redemption ran into the caves, ran into the hollow darkness because they couldn't bear to look at each other. It is assumed that depression overtook them and grief soured their hearts. Oh the shame and hurt that they felt in their inner man as they had broken correspondence with their precious Father and purpose.

Family, redemption has come and a new tree of life was erected in the middle of history. The Cross of Christ stands tall above great philosophies that may free a man's conscience but keeps his heart bound. A garden has been built around that glorious tree, a gate opened but accessed by a narrow path. A road of which we have strayed, a road we no longer encourage for the wayward souls of our new and needing brothers and sisters. We have glorified the road that leads to the lake of fire and diminished the road that leads to Him.

Many of us were found in the hollow hallways of darkness, a light shined dimly at the entrance of the gate and there two paths have presented itself. A narrow and seemingly long path and the wide and seemingly short path. There, the great evangelist stands at the entrance of the narrow path shouting into the caves of bitter death, "Come, repent, leave the darkness and walk with me back to the tree of life. Back to the glory and intimate proximity with The Father." He cried, " Rebel against the darkness, rebel against the voice of death and ignore the voice of the preachers of the wide path." He beckons us and calls unto us to the walk of a lifetime. He calls to sanctify you and keep you sanctified. He calls to make you new and keep you new. He calls to make you guiltless and keep you guiltless. He calls to fill you with love and keep you filled. The only thing that keeps you from Him is to rebel against the darkness and run after Him— what keeps you from Him is repentance.

At the second path, the wide and seemingly short, there many preachers have gathered against him and stand at its entrances also crying into the darkened caves. Crying in a similar benevolent tone. Calling men to self justification, self given grace and forgiveness. They extend the cheapened mercy and glory in His death and not His resurrection. They preach the one who has died, and lives only to extend grace unto a blinded eye and seared conscience of things that grieve His heart. They preach His death without resurrection, leaving Jesus's sacrifice as the primary entrance key yet reject the resurrected Lord on the other side of the true testimony demands the life worthy of His cross. They beckon men in partnership with the darkened slave master to keep them bound and in deceptive ecstasy, only to the quick plunge into to lake under the cliff in which they walk towards. They come out of the cave, thinking they have received forgiveness without repentance, that they can take the balls and chains that their darkened slave master had given them and unaware they have become attendants of the great procession to hell.

What grief has the Lamb, as the preachers of His imposter steals the sheep He has gone out so far himself to find and redeem. What anger kindles in His heart and great jealousy have we stirred up within Him. Within the mystery of His patience and urgency of His judgement He shouts to the simpletons that stand at the great wide gates to also repent and return unto Him. He shouts to us as He did in generations past, "Turn to Me with all your heart, With fasting, with weeping, and with mourning." Return to the Lord your God, For He is gracious and merciful, Slow to anger, and of great kindness; And He relents from doing harm.

Preacher, an hour of repentance has been extended to us. The true Christ speaks to your hearts and shouts into your studies and bedrooms. He speaks in your hotel rooms, and in the lavish cars you ride as you pompously enjoy the indulgences of fleshly honor, calling it His blessings, yet your hearts are far from Him and cold. He speaks as you read, bring awareness of His goodness and kindness. He calls you preachers to bow your knee, to turn from the wide paths, turn from the imposter and yet again yield to Him. "See that you do not refuse him who is speaking. For if they did not escape when they refused him who warned them on earth, much less will we escape if we reject him who warns from heaven."[2] The hour of His benevolence is upon us. Hear him now and not then in judgement. Turn while there is a chance. Repent. Rebel against the wide paths that you have paved for yourself and many others. Return to "the gospel of the glory of the blessed God."[3] The kingdom is at hand. Repent. The kingdom is at hand. For once more He says, "I will shake not only the earth but also the heavens."[4] "See to it that [you] fail not to obtain the grace of God."[5] He who has an ear, let him hear what the Spirit says.

Do you now hear the Lord's mercy, as He calls unto us again. When the word of the Lord came to us in August of 2015 it was spoken, "Within this coming time, there is a holy confrontation ordained for the Church. The Lord is visiting our churches, sitting in our pews, listening to our messages, for the plumb line has been sent from heaven and the vinedresser is here to judge our fruit and our fruitfulness." The fear of the Lord was heavy upon us and the grace to respond forceful. The song upon our lips sang of His mercy and endurance with us. And again that same song rise from my own heart. For my trust lies in the Father's declaration, "As many as I love, I rebuke and chasten."[6] Oh the love of God for us. I've heard what the Spirit has to say and conviction has worked me through.

The word of the Lord has come to you and the grace to respond is near. The Lord has spoken, what is there to say but thank you. Messages like these aren't meant for condemnation, but self-examination. I am convinced it is not I who says these thing, for the same words lit the same lamp that continues even now to search my own soul. These days have been filled with great sorrow and fear at the word of the Lord to us. Yet my heart has rejoiced in gladness as the Lord is reconciling us to His ways and the knowledge of His heart.

Rebuke is not unto death, nor is it unto hell. Rebuke coupled with the right response only results in reconciliation. David once spoke, "The Lord has chastened me severely, But He has not given me over to death."[7] Because it is so, we must not "despise the chastening of the Lord, nor detest His correction; for whom the Lord loves He corrects, just as a father the son in whom he delights."[8] Our Father the Lord Sovereign is speaking to us plainly. Not with many pages or many words. But with words that beckon us to action. That beckons us to the right response. I sit here in grief, asking the Lord to save the souls of those who read this. That you have not turned away from the Lord nor given yourself to the hardness of heart. I implore you to search your heart, for this book is drenched in the love of God for us. These words have sprung up from the well of His kindness. Know that he has not forsaken the humble, nor will he resist those that bow the knee. For the rebuke is to reconcile. He desires not to reconcile with a people that will not pursue and walk in His ways and esteem Him as He must. He who has an ear, let him hear what the Spirit says.

Endnotes

1. Joel 2:12-14 (NKJV). The Lord's call for whole-hearted repentance involving fasting, weeping, and mourning—not mere external ritual but true heart transformation, based on His merciful and gracious character.
2. Hebrews 12:25 (NKJV). The author's warning not to refuse Christ who speaks from heaven, emphasizing that rejecting His heavenly voice brings far greater consequences than rejecting earthly messengers.
3. 1 Timothy 1:11 (NKJV). Paul's reference to the glorious gospel of the blessed God, emphasizing the true nature of the gospel message versus false presentations of it.
4. Hebrews 12:26 (NKJV). The promise of God to shake not only the earth but also the heavens, indicating the comprehensive nature of divine judgment and the removal of all that can be shaken.
5. Hebrews 12:15 (NKJV). The warning to see that no one fails to obtain the grace of God, emphasizing the urgency of responding to God's offer of mercy and forgiveness during the hour of opportunity.
6. Revelation 3:19 (NKJV). Christ's explanation that His rebuke and chastening of the lukewarm church springs from His love, demonstrating that divine correction is evidence of divine affection.
7. Psalm 118:18 (NKJV). David's testimony that though the Lord chastened him severely, He did not give him over to death, showing that divine discipline aims at correction, not destruction.
8. Proverbs 3:11-12 (NKJV). Solomon's wisdom about not despising the Lord's chastening, understanding that whom the Lord loves He corrects, just as a father corrects the son in whom he delights.

Holiness in the Pulpit

A holy God demands holy preachers. The holiness of the Lord fills the heavens and to represent him the holiness of God must fill your hearts. John, baptizing the people unto repentance in preparation for the Messiah saw afar the Pharisees and scribes. They seemed like they were doing a great thing yet they kindled a fire of indignation within John. He shouted, "Brood of vipers! Who warned you to flee from the wrath to come? Therefore bear fruits worthy of repentance.."[1] Oh the sword that pierced their anger as they are humiliated before men. John demanded that they not only come to the altar in repentance if they haven't intended to live a life worthy of repentance. Many will claim to have repented but cease to bear the fruits worthy of repentance. Many will not be ready to walk on the highway of holiness. But preachers, if you are to continue after repentance, if you are to be saved from the wrath our sins have heaped up for us, you have no choice but to live a holy life.

Holiness is not a option within the kingdom and servant-hood of God. It is a command. It is written, "Be holy, for I am holy."[2] And moreover you preachers must for our eternity is in the balance, for "let not many of you become teachers, knowing that we shall receive a stricter judgment."[3] It is a weighty cause to take up the role of a preacher of God. We have become so comfortable with the Lord, we have treated the servanthood disrespectful. Preaching is now an art, the prophetic is a game, teachers are now self-help gurus and apostles think they are makers of destinies. It is because of holiness Jeremiah trembled, saying, "My heart within me is broken Because of the prophets; All my bones shake. I am like a drunken man, and like a man whom wine has overcome, because of the Lord, and because of His holy words."[4] It is because of holiness Isaiah noticed the condition of His soul crying, ""Woe is me, for I am undone! Because I am a man of unclean lips."[5] He knew he was ruined. He was done for. He was found lacking in the presence of holiness. We have not yet seen the glory of God in our churches. We have experienced brooding but never a full landing of the Spirit walking amongst us. For if truly the Spirit of holiness step foot on our floors or our platforms conviction would capture every heart and the fear of the Lord would grip us.

I am convinced we have yet to encounter the true Christ for when John saw Him he "fell at His feet as dead."[6] And seeing the same Christ pre-incarnate, men fled for terror and Daniel hearing His words found, "no strength remained in me; for my vigor was turned to frailty in me, and I retained no strength...I was in a deep sleep on my face, with my face to the ground."[7] The Christ we serve is to be fear. We think because we giggle to the floor we have experienced the essence of God. Yet we rise void of the fear of the Lord. For the fear of the Lord is the beginning of holiness. It speaks of the ministry of Christ saying, "The Spirit of the Lord shall rest upon Him, The Spirit of wisdom and understanding, The Spirit of counsel and might, The Spirit of knowledge and of the fear of the Lord. His delight is in the fear of the Lord..."[8] The fear of the the Lord is the Holy Spirit and the delight of Christ was in the fear of the Lord. Jesus said, "My food is to do the will of Him who sent Me, and to finish His work."[9] The fear of the Lord made Christ's diet obedience.

It is written that Christ was, "declared to be the Son of God with power according to the Spirit of holiness"[10] If Christ was identified by His holiness, we must also be identified by our holiness. Many preachers have walked behind a pulpit with dynamics in their minds and a plan on when to holler. But the true power of the ministry is found within holiness. Power is according to holiness. Christ was declared the Son of God with power, not by His meticulous exegesis. He spoke with power and healed the sick with power because He was holy. Preacher, if you are to ever be a servant of the true living God, you must be holy. Because no servant of God has ever seen the power that heals the sick, or raised the dead without first burning with the flames of holiness.

It is holiness that settles the brooding Spirit. Samson was born under a vow to be holy before the Lord and as an expression of his holiness he was never to drink wine or cut his hair. When Samson grew of age, it is said, "the Lord blessed him. And the Spirit of the Lord began to move upon him."[11] As long as Samson stayed holy, "the Spirit of the Lord came mightily upon him."[12] But when same step from the canopy of holiness by the hands of his wife the Spirit of the Lord never returned and Samson. Even when he repented in captivity of the Philistines and willed the kill them all but He did it, "with all his might."[13]

One of the many reasons the Spirit may not be able to rest amongst you preachers, in the pulpit or in your communities is because of the holiness factor. The command remains, " Pursue...holiness, without which no one will see the Lord."[14] Do not assume because you stand and audience to their that the Spirit of God was upon you. The unction, the burden of the Lord is only expressed through holy preachers and you may be able to fool men with charisma, but before God every sermon in sin is being counted against you.

You say, "Caleb, you sound like you are asking me to be prefect but it is impossible." Family, do you perfection is a commandment of Christ. He spoke from His own lips, "Therefore you shall be perfect, just as your Father in heaven is perfect."[15] How do you answer that? Do you just brush the Lord off and say its impossible? Why are you still "behaving like mere men?"[16] In answer to the weakness in our lives the Lord has said to us, "My grace is sufficient for you, for My strength is made perfect in weakness."[17] Yet we deafen our ears because we rather not see that a holy and perfect is not work forth through good deeds, it is worked forth repentance.

True repentance is unto maturity. Scripture states, "in it the righteousness of God is revealed from faith to faith."[18] For, "by that will we have been sanctified through the offering of the body of Jesus Christ once for all."[19] Faith in the work of the Cross has made us holy and perfect before God, yet it is grace that is to maintain it. We have the Spirit of grace not just upon us but within us. Holiness worked from by the Spirit. The Spirit was the one that enabled Jesus to present, "himself without blemish to God."[20] And it is by that same Spirit, we also will have power to "be kept blameless at the coming of our Lord Jesus Christ."[21] Yet holiness has be pursued. Holiness is a consequence of Christ's cross, its maintenance is the consequence of our pursuits.

"Be holy as I am holy" preacher, is the commandment. Being holy isn't a badge it is a key. If we desire to see heaven in the earth, we must be baptized in the essence of God—holiness. He who has an ear, let him hear what the Spirit says.

Endnotes

1. Matthew 3:7-8 (NKJV). John the Baptist's fierce rebuke of the religious leaders, demanding not just verbal repentance but fruit that demonstrates genuine life change.
2. 1 Peter 1:16 (NKJV). God's command for His people to be holy as He is holy, establishing holiness not as an option but as a divine requirement for those who would serve Him.
3. James 3:1 (NKJV). James' warning that teachers and preachers face stricter judgment, emphasizing the weight of responsibility that comes with spiritual leadership.
4. Jeremiah 23:9 (NKJV). Jeremiah's description of how his heart was broken and his bones shook because of the holiness of God and His holy words, demonstrating the prophet's reverential fear.
5. Isaiah 6:5 (NKJV). Isaiah's cry of being undone when he encountered the holiness of God, recognizing his own sinfulness in the presence of absolute purity.
6. Revelation 1:17 (NKJV). John's reaction to seeing the glorified Christ—falling as dead at His feet—demonstrating the overwhelming effect of encountering divine glory.
7. Daniel 10:8-9 (NKJV). Daniel's complete physical collapse when encountering the pre-incarnate Christ, showing how divine presence affects human flesh.
8. Isaiah 11:2-3 (NKJV). The sevenfold Spirit of the Lord that would rest upon the Messiah, including the Spirit of the fear of the Lord, and noting that Christ's delight was in the fear of the Lord.
9. John 4:34 (NKJV). Jesus' declaration that His food was to do the will of the Father and finish His work, showing how fear of the Lord produces perfect obedience.

10. Romans 1:4 (NKJV). Paul's statement that Christ was declared to be the Son of God with power according to the Spirit of holiness, connecting divine power with holiness.

11. Judges 13:24-25 (NKJV). The record of how the Lord blessed Samson and the Spirit began to move upon him while he maintained his Nazarite vow of holiness.

12. Judges 14:6, 15:14 (NKJV). Examples of how the Spirit of the Lord came mightily upon Samson during his period of holiness, enabling supernatural strength and victory.

13. Judges 16:28-30 (NKJV). Samson's final act was done with "all his might"—human strength alone—rather than the supernatural empowerment of the Spirit which had departed when his holiness was compromised.

14. Hebrews 12:14 (NKJV). The author's command to pursue holiness, without which no one will see the Lord, establishing holiness as essential for divine encounter and ministry.

15. Matthew 5:48 (NKJV). Jesus' command for His followers to be perfect as the heavenly Father is perfect, establishing divine perfection as the standard and goal.

16. 1 Corinthians 3:3 (NKJV). Paul's rebuke to the Corinthians for behaving like mere men rather than spirit-empowered believers, indicating that carnality contradicts Christian identity.

17. 2 Corinthians 12:9 (NKJV). Christ's promise that His grace is sufficient and His strength is made perfect in weakness, showing how divine power enables what seems humanly impossible.

18. Romans 1:17 (NKJV). The progressive revelation of God's righteousness from faith to faith, indicating the ongoing process of spiritual maturity and holiness.

19. Hebrews 10:10 (NKJV). The once-for-all sanctification achieved through Christ's offering, establishing the foundation upon which ongoing holiness is built.

20. Hebrews 9:14 (NKJV). The eternal Spirit enabled Christ to offer Himself without blemish to God, demonstrating the role of the Spirit in maintaining perfect holiness.
21. 1 Thessalonians 5:23-24 (NKJV). Paul's prayer for complete sanctification and God's faithfulness to keep believers blameless, showing divine power available for maintaining holiness.

Bibliography

Bonhoeffer, Dietrich. *The Cost of Discipleship*. New York: Macmillan, 1959.

Bounds, E.M. *Power Through Prayer*. Grand Rapids: Zondervan, 1991.

Comfort, Ray. *God Has a Wonderful Plan for Your Life: The Myth of the Modern Message*. Bellflower, CA: Living Waters Publications, 2010.

Edwards, Jonathan. "Sinners in the Hands of an Angry God." Sermon preached at Enfield, Connecticut, July 8, 1741.

Ravenhill, Leonard. *Revival God's Way: A Message for the Church*. Minneapolis: Bethany House, 1983.

———. *Why Revival Tarries*. Minneapolis: Bethany House, 2004.

Spurgeon, Charles H. *Metropolitan Tabernacle Pulpit*. Vol. 42. London: Passmore & Alabaster, 1896.

Tozer, A.W. *God Tells the Man Who Cares*. Harrisburg, PA: Christian Publications, 1970.

———. *The Knowledge of the Holy*. New York: Harper & Row, 1961.

———. *Of God and Men*. Harrisburg, PA: Christian Publications, 1960.

———. *Whatever Happened to Worship?* Camp Hill, PA: Christian Publications, 1985.

Willard, Dallas. *The Divine Conspiracy: Rediscovering Our Hidden Life in God*. San Francisco: HarperCollins, 1998.

———. *Renovation of the Heart: Putting On the Character of Christ*. Colorado Springs: NavPress, 2002.